How to Start a Business for Teens

The Teenager's Complete Guide to Financial Self-sufficiency at a Young Age

Candace B. Marrigold

DISCLAIMER

How to Start a Business for Teens: The Teenager's Complete Guide to Financial Self-sufficiency at a Young Age

First edition.

TABLE OF CONTENTS

PART 1

Igniting Your Entrepreneurial Spark

INTRODUCTION

THE ADVANTAGES OF TEEN ENTREPRENEURSHIP

The teenage years are a time of exploration, discovery, and forging your own path. While many teenagers yearn for greater independence, financial dependence on parents often remains a reality. However, embarking on the exciting journey of teen entrepreneurship offers a unique opportunity to achieve financial independence and responsibility at a young age. This chapter delves into the numerous advantages of teen entrepreneurship, highlighting how it empowers you to take control of your finances and build a solid foundation for your future.

Financial Independence

Financial independence is the cornerstone of freedom and self-reliance. As a teen entrepreneur, your business becomes a vehicle for generating your own income. This income allows you to:

- **Cover Your Expenses:** Imagine the satisfaction of paying for your phone bill, clothes, or entertainment with money you earned through your own hard work and initiative. Teen entrepreneurship empowers you to manage your personal finances with a sense of accomplishment and ownership.
- **Pursue Your Passions:** Financial independence grants you the freedom to explore your interests and invest in your passions. This could be attending workshops related to your business, buying equipment to enhance your skills, or even taking a small vacation to recharge and spark new ideas.
- **Contribute to the Household:** While not an obligation, earning your own income allows you to

contribute to household expenses, easing the burden on your parents and fostering a sense of responsibility within the family unit.

- **Build Savings and Investments:** The income generated from your business becomes a powerful tool for financial planning. You can set aside money for future goals like college education, a dream vacation, or even a down payment on a car. Early savings and investments have the potential to grow significantly over time, giving you a head start in building long-term wealth.

Financial Responsibility

Financial responsibility is a valuable life skill, and teen entrepreneurship provides a real-world learning environment. Running your own business exposes you to various financial concepts, fostering a deeper understanding and appreciation for:

- **Budgeting:** The success of your business hinges on managing your finances effectively. You'll learn to allocate funds for supplies, marketing, and potential reinvestments, understanding the importance of living within your means.
- **Profit and Loss:** Teen entrepreneurship offers a firsthand experience with the concept of profit and loss. You'll see how your pricing strategies and operational costs impact your bottom line, teaching you valuable lessons about managing income and expenses.
- **Saving and Investing:** As your business grows, you'll likely encounter situations where reinvesting profits becomes essential for expansion or improvement. This gives you a practical understanding of the power of saving and investing, a skillset that will benefit you throughout your life.

- **Taxes:** While seemingly complex, understanding basic tax principles is crucial for any entrepreneur. You'll learn about filing taxes for your business, familiarizing yourself with tax deductions and obligations. This early exposure lays the groundwork for responsible tax management in the future.

Developing a Strong Work Ethic and Confidence

Running a business demands dedication, hard work, and perseverance. Teen entrepreneurship fosters a strong work ethic, encouraging you to set goals, manage your time effectively, and overcome challenges with grit and determination. As you witness your business grow and your efforts translate into success, your confidence soars. You develop a sense of self-belief and an "I can do it" attitude that becomes invaluable in all aspects of life.

Learning Valuable Business Skills

Teen entrepreneurship is more than just about making money; it's an immersive learning experience. By launching your own venture, you gain valuable business skills that will benefit you throughout your life, including:

- **Marketing and Sales:** You'll learn how to effectively market your product or service to your target audience, understanding the importance of branding, communication, and customer engagement.
- **Problem-Solving:** Running a business inevitably throws curveballs your way. As a teen entrepreneur, you'll develop your problem-solving skills, learning to think critically, adapt to changing circumstances, and find creative solutions to challenges.
- **Customer Service:** Building a loyal customer base is essential for any business. You'll learn the importance of excellent customer service, fostering communication

skills and building strong relationships with your clientele.

- **Decision-Making:** Every day as an entrepreneur involves making crucial decisions. This experience hones your decision-making skills, encouraging you to weigh options, analyze risks, and make informed choices for the success of your business.

Networking and Building Relationships

The entrepreneurial journey is not a solitary path. Teen entrepreneurs have the opportunity to network with other young business owners, mentors, and potential investors. These connections can open doors to new ideas, collaborations, and even future job opportunities. You'll develop valuable communication and interpersonal skills as you connect with others in the business world. These connections can become a strong support system, offering guidance, encouragement, and a sense of community.

Exploring Your Passions and Discovering Your Path

Many teenagers grapple with questions about their future careers. Teen entrepreneurship allows you to explore your interests in a practical way. By turning a passion into a business, you gain firsthand experience in that field, helping you discover if it aligns with your long-term aspirations. This early exploration allows you to refine your career goals and make more informed decisions about your future education and professional path.

Building a Strong Portfolio and Standing Out From the Crowd

There are few things in the business world more impressive than a teenager who is an entrepreneur, whether in the job market, in your academics or elsewhere. Your entrepreneurial experience, regardless of its success or setbacks, becomes a valuable asset on your resume.

Having a business to showcase on college applications or job interviews demonstrates initiative, leadership, and a strong work ethic. The skills you acquired, from marketing to problem-solving, are highly sought-after by employers. This unique experience sets you apart from other applicants, giving you a competitive edge in your future endeavors.

In the end, the decision to embark on the journey of teen entrepreneurship is not just about making money today; it's about investing in your future. By taking control of your finances, developing valuable skills, and building a strong work ethic, you pave the way for a brighter tomorrow. The financial independence and responsibility you cultivate as a teen entrepreneur will serve you well throughout your life, empowering you to achieve your goals and build a secure and fulfilling future.

CHAPTER 1
UNLEASHING YOUR BUSINESS IDEA

IDENTIFYING YOUR SKILLS AND PASSIONS

The world of business thrives on a potent blend: a fiery passion for a pursuit intertwined with the skilled hands that can bring it to life. As a teen entrepreneur, identifying your unique strengths and interests is the crucial first step in crafting a successful business idea.

Discovering Your Skills

Think of your skills as the tools in your entrepreneurial toolbox. They are the strengths you possess that allow you to excel in specific areas. But how do you identify them? Here's how to embark on a treasure hunt within:

- **Reflect on Past Achievements:** Take a trip down memory lane. Think about school projects, extracurricular activities, or hobbies where you excelled. What skills did you utilize in those situations? Did you demonstrate leadership qualities by spearheading a group project, or maybe your artistic skills shone through in a school play or competition? Recalling past successes can shed light on your strengths.
- **Seek Feedback from Others:** Don't be afraid to ask for a hand in uncovering your hidden talents. Seek honest input from teachers, coaches, parents, and friends. What skills do they see in you? This external perspective can highlight strengths you might have overlooked. Perhaps a friend consistently compliments your organization skills, or a teacher recognizes your

natural ability to explain complex concepts. These observations can be invaluable clues.

- **Take Online Assessments:** Several free online skills assessments are available to provide valuable insights. These tools might evaluate communication skills, problem-solving abilities, or analytical thinking. While these assessments can't be the sole measure of your strengths, they can offer starting points for further exploration.

Categorizing Your Skills: There are two main categories of skills that will be crucial for your entrepreneurial journey: hard skills and soft skills. Hard skills are teachable and often involve technical knowledge, such as graphic design, computer programming, or foreign languages. Mastering these skills allows you to perform specific tasks effectively.

Soft skills, on the other hand, are not as easily quantifiable. They are personality traits and interpersonal abilities that contribute to your overall success in interacting with others and navigating various situations. Communication, teamwork, leadership, creativity, and critical thinking are all examples of soft skills.

While both hard and soft skills are valuable, soft skills are often considered foundational for entrepreneurial success. After all, a business owner who can't communicate effectively with customers or build strong relationships with collaborators is unlikely to thrive.

Exploring Your Passions

Passion is the fuel that ignites your entrepreneurial journey. It's the driving force that keeps you motivated and enthusiastic, even when faced with challenges. Imagine venturing into a business you find utterly mundane. The initial spark of excitement might quickly fizzle out, leaving you feeling uninspired and unmotivated. Here are some ways to identify your passions:

- **Consider Activities You Lose Track of Time Doing:** What hobbies or activities bring you immense joy and satisfaction? Do you lose track of time getting lost in a good book, creating art, or playing a musical instrument? These activities might hold a deep-seated passion waiting to be explored. Perhaps you spend hours researching historical topics, hinting at a passion for history that could translate into a blog or even a historical walking tour business.
- **Imagine Your Dream Job:** If limitations weren't a factor, what would your ideal job look like? Would you spend your days writing, designing clothes, or working with animals? Delving into your fantasy dream job can reveal hidden passions. Maybe you envision yourself constantly traveling and writing about different cultures, hinting at a passion for travel and writing that could be channeled into a travel blog or freelance writing service.
- **Look for Patterns in Your Interests:** Do you gravitate towards specific genres of books or movies? Are you drawn to historical documentaries or action-packed thrillers? Identifying patterns in your entertainment choices can reveal underlying passions and areas of interest. Perhaps you're fascinated by true crime podcasts, hinting at a passion for research and storytelling that could be channeled into a true crime podcast of your own.

Blending Passion and Skill

The magic truly happens when you find the intersection between your skills and passions. This sweet spot is where your business idea ignites. Imagine you have a passion for baking and possess strong organizational skills. You could start a small bakery business, utilizing your baking skills to create delicious treats while your organizational skills ensure efficient production and inventory management. The combination of your passion for baking and your organizational skills creates a strong foundation for a successful venture.

Here are some strategies to explore the convergence of passion and skill:

- **Brainstorm Business Ideas that Align with Your Skills:** Consider what products or services you could create or offer that leverage your existing skillset. Can you use your graphic design skills to create logos for local businesses or design eye-catching posters for community events? Perhaps your talent for writing can translate into a freelance content writing service or even a blog focused on a specific niche you're passionate about.

- **Think About How Your Passions Can Be Monetized:** Is there a way to translate your passion for photography into a business offering photo editing services or event photography? If you love animals, could you start a pet-sitting or dog-walking service, or even create a blog offering pet care tips and tricks?
- **Combine Your Skills and Passions in Unexpected Ways:** Don't be afraid to get creative. Maybe your passion for music and your coding skills can lead to developing a music education app. Perhaps your love for fashion and your talent for writing can be channeled into a blog that reviews sustainable clothing brands. The possibilities are endless, and the most successful business ideas often emerge from unexpected combinations of skills and passions.

In all this it is important that you bear in mind the following:

- **There's No Single "Right" Passion:** Don't limit yourself by societal expectations. Your passion could be anything from baking delicious cookies to playing video games competitively. What matters is that it sparks your enthusiasm and motivates you to keep going, even when faced with challenges.
- **Passion Can Be Cultivated:** Not everything you're passionate about will come naturally. If you have an interest in a particular field, you can nurture that passion by learning new skills and immersing yourself in the subject matter. Perhaps you're intrigued by the world of finance but lack the technical knowledge. You can take online courses, read books on investing, or even shadow a financial advisor to develop the skills needed to potentially start a business related to finance.
- **Don't Be Afraid to Experiment:** The initial business idea might not be your final one. As you explore and learn, your skills and passions might evolve, leading you to refine your idea or discover an entirely new path. Embrace the journey of self-discovery and allow your exploration to guide you. Identifying your skills and passions is an exciting adventure of self-discovery. This initial exploration might not yield a fully formed business plan just yet, but it lays the groundwork for a successful venture. With a clear understanding of your strengths and the areas that ignite your spirit, you can approach the brainstorming process with focus and purpose.

SPOTTING MARKET GAPS AND OPPORTUNITIES

There is one principle that always works as regards business: **The biggest profits will always be made by solving the biggest needs**. As an example, let's look at one of the most basic needs that humans have: the need to feed. This need has made the food industries to be one of the most successful industries ever. Another example is the need for accommodation: this has made the real estate industry and rental businesses like Airbnb to be one the biggest and most successful in the world. The list goes on endlessly, but I'm sure you've gotten my point.

The world of business thrives on innovation and fulfilling unmet needs. As a budding teen entrepreneur, your ability to identify gaps in the current market can be the cornerstone of your success. It can be what will separate you from being just another person trying to make a quick buck and someone who will be successful and stand out. This is what we will be discussing in this section.

Understanding Market Gaps:

A market gap exists when there's a mismatch between what consumers need or want and what businesses are currently offering. This gap could be a product that doesn't exist, a service that's inconvenient or inaccessible, or even a lack of awareness about a particular need.

Here are some reasons why market gaps emerge:

- **Changing Consumer Needs:** Society is constantly evolving, and consumer needs and preferences shift with it. New technologies, changing lifestyles, and environmental concerns can all create new market gaps.
- **Limited Product Selection:** Existing businesses might offer a limited range of products or services, leaving room for niche options that cater to specific consumer preferences.
- **Poor Customer Service:** If current businesses are not providing a satisfactory customer service

experience, there's an opportunity for a new venture to prioritize excellent customer care and build a loyal following.

- **Geographic Inaccessibility:** Certain products or services might not be readily available in specific locations, creating an opportunity for a local business to fill the gap.

Developing Your Observation Skills:

Becoming a master of spotting market gaps requires keen observation skills. Here are some ways to hone your ability to identify unmet needs:

- **Become an Active Consumer:** Pay close attention to your own experiences as a consumer. Are there any products or services that consistently disappoint you? What frustrations do you encounter when dealing with established businesses?
- **Talk to People:** Engage in conversations with friends, family, and even strangers. Ask them about their daily struggles, what products they wish existed, and what aspects of existing services they find frustrating.
- **Stay Informed:** Keep up-to-date with current trends and news in your local community and beyond. Are there any emerging technologies or social movements that could create new needs?
- **Explore Social Media:** Social media platforms are valuable tools for gauging consumer sentiment. Look for online communities where people discuss their frustrations and unmet needs.

Identifying Opportunities Within the Gaps:

Once you've identified a market gap, the next step is to assess its potential for a successful business venture. Here are some questions to consider:

- **Is There a Large Enough Target Market?:** Is the gap big enough to support a viable business? While a niche market can be profitable, a very narrow audience might not generate enough revenue for long-term success.
- **Is There Competition?:** Even if a gap exists, are there already businesses attempting to fill it? If so, what are their strengths and weaknesses? Can you offer a unique selling proposition (USP) that sets you apart?
- **Is it a Viable Business Model?:** Can you develop a business model that allows you to offer your product or service profitably? Consider your production costs, pricing strategy, and target profit margins.

Examples of Market Gaps:

Here are some examples to spark your imagination and showcase the diverse possibilities:

- **Environmentally-Conscious Products:** Many teenagers are passionate about sustainability. There might be a gap in the market for eco-friendly products like reusable alternatives to single-use plastics or clothing made from recycled materials.
- **Tech-Savvy Services:** Teenagers are often comfortable with technology. Could you offer tech support services to older generations or create educational resources to help people learn new digital skills?
- **Local Needs:** Your local community might have specific needs that aren't being met. Perhaps there's a lack of delivery services for healthy meals or a need for pet walking services catering to busy families.
- **Entertainment Options:** Teenagers are a valuable target audience for entertainment options. Is there a gap in your community for after-school activities,

workshops focused on specific interests, or even unique entertainment events for teenagers?

To be able to effectively spot wants and needs that need to be satisfied, wants and needs that you will be able to satisfy without breaking any laws, be sure to incorporate the following into your practice:

- **Think Outside the Box:** Don't be afraid to come up with unconventional ideas. Some of the most successful businesses started by filling gaps that others simply overlooked.
- **Start Small and Scale Up:** You don't need a revolutionary product or service to launch a successful business. Start by filling a small gap in your local market and then scale up based on demand.
- **Validate Your Idea:** Before investing significant time and resources, test your business idea with your target market. Conduct surveys, gather feedback, and see if there's genuine interest in what you're offering.

The ability to spot market gaps and opportunities is a valuable skill for any entrepreneur, but especially for teenagers entering the business world. By honing your observation skills, staying informed about trends, and actively seeking out unmet needs, you can identify a niche that perfectly aligns with your skills and passions.

Remember that successful businesses often address a problem or frustration that others have simply grown accustomed to. With a keen eye, a creative mind, and the willingness to take action, you can transform a market gap into a thriving business.

BRAINSTORMING CREATIVE BUSINESS CONCEPTS

Before diving into brainstorming strategies, it's crucial to cultivate a creative mindset. Here are some tips to get your creative juices flowing:

- **Embrace Playfulness:** Shed inhibitions and approach brainstorming with a playful spirit. Don't be afraid to explore unconventional ideas, even if they seem silly at first. Often, the most groundbreaking ideas emerge from a playful exploration of possibilities. Remember the story of Silly Putty? Created by a scientist experimenting with new rubber compounds, it was initially considered a failed experiment. Today, it's a beloved toy enjoyed by millions.
- **Challenge Assumptions:** Question the status quo. Don't take things at face value. Ask yourself, "Is there a better way to do this?" For example, the music industry was once dominated by record labels controlling distribution. Then came Napster, a peer-to-peer file-sharing platform that challenged the traditional model and paved the way for streaming services like Spotify and Apple Music.
- **Surround Yourself with Inspiration:** Seek out environments that inspire creativity. Visit museums, art galleries, or attend industry events. Immerse yourself in books, podcasts, or documentaries that delve into innovation and successful startups. Steve Jobs, co-founder of Apple, was known for his frequent visits to Xerox PARC, a research facility known for its groundbreaking innovations. These visits undoubtedly influenced his vision for personal computers.
- **Collaborate with Others:** Brainstorming with friends, family, or even mentors can spark new ideas and perspectives. Bounce ideas off each other, build upon each other's suggestions, and create a synergy of

creative energy. The co-founders of Ben & Jerry's ice cream met in college and began experimenting with flavors in their dorm room. Their playful collaboration led to a brand known for its unique and delicious ice cream creations.

Brainstorming Techniques for Budding Entrepreneurs:

Now that you've cultivated a creative mindset, let's explore some brainstorming techniques specifically tailored for aspiring teen entrepreneurs:

- **Mind Mapping:** Create a visual representation of your central idea. Draw a circle in the center of a page and write your business concept within it. Then, branch out with lines connecting all the different aspects of your business, including potential products or services, target market, and marketing strategies. This technique allows you to see how different elements interconnect and fosters the generation of new ideas. Imagine you're brainstorming a business concept for a healthy snack delivery service for students. Your mind map might include branches for different snack options, dietary restrictions you can cater to, delivery methods, potential partnerships with local bakeries or health food stores, and even marketing strategies like social media campaigns aimed at busy students.
- **The 5 Whys:** This technique encourages you to delve deeper into a problem or need. Start with a problem you've identified in your target market (e.g., teenagers often struggle to find healthy and affordable lunch options at school). Ask yourself "Why" this is a problem. The answer might reveal a potential business opportunity (e.g., there's a need for a healthy and convenient lunch delivery service targeted at students).

Repeat the "Why" question five times, each time uncovering a deeper layer of the problem and potentially leading you to a more innovative solution. For instance, after identifying the need for healthy school lunches, you might ask "Why" students struggle with this. The answer could be limited access to healthy options in the cafeteria or a lack of time to prepare lunches at home. This deeper understanding can help you tailor your lunch delivery service to address these specific challenges.

- **SCAMPER:** This acronym stands for Substitute, Combine, Adapt, Modify, Put to a Different Use, Eliminate, and Reverse. Use these prompts to explore your initial business idea from different angles. For example, if your idea is to create a custom phone case business (Substitute), could you combine it with a platform for young artists to design the cases (Combine)? Perhaps you could modify your idea to offer phone cases made from recycled materials (Modify) or explore ways to eliminate the need for phone cases altogether by developing a protective phone coating service (Eliminate).
- **Random Word Inspiration:** Pick two random words from a dictionary or online generator. Challenge yourself to brainstorm how these seemingly unrelated words could be used together to create a new business concept. Perhaps the words "origami" and "smartphone" could spark an idea for a unique and foldable phone stand that utilizes origami principles. The possibilities are endless, and the key is to embrace the unexpected connections that can emerge.

Finding Inspiration in Your Surroundings:

Your daily life is brimming with potential business ideas. Here are some ways to find inspiration in your surroundings:

- **Identify Your Personal Pain Points:** What aspects of your daily life are inconvenient, frustrating, or simply lacking? Is there a product or service that would make your life easier or more enjoyable? Often, the problems you encounter are also faced by others, presenting potential business opportunities. For instance, you might struggle to find high-quality, affordable textbooks for your classes. This could spark an idea for a peer-to-peer textbook exchange platform where students can buy and sell used textbooks directly from each other.
- **Observe Community Needs:** Pay close attention to the needs and challenges within your local community. Are there specific demographics that are underserved? Is there a lack of resources or activities for teenagers in your area? Identifying these gaps can lead to impactful business ideas that benefit your community. Perhaps you notice a lack of after-school programs for younger children in your neighborhood. This could inspire you to start a business offering tutoring or enrichment activities for younger students.
- **Embrace Current Trends:** Stay informed about current trends and social movements. Can you leverage these trends to create a product or service that caters to emerging needs and interests? For example, the growing interest in sustainability could inspire a business offering eco-friendly pet care products or a dog walking service that uses electric bikes for transportation.
- **Reverse Engineer Existing Businesses:** Take a closer look at successful businesses and ask yourself, "How could I adapt this model to a different market or a new need?" For instance, the subscription box model popularized by companies like Birchbox could be adapted to cater to teenagers, offering curated boxes of beauty products, art supplies, or even healthy snacks.

Evaluating Your Ideas:

Once you've generated a plethora of business ideas, it's time to assess their potential. Here are some questions to consider:

- **Passion and Skills Alignment:** Does this business idea align with your passions and skills? Are you excited about the prospect of working on this venture long-term? Remember that passion is a powerful fuel that will keep you motivated through challenges. If you're not passionate about your business idea, it might be difficult to sustain your enthusiasm over time.
- **Market Need and Competition:** Is there a genuine need for this product or service in your target market? Who are your potential competitors, and what is their unique selling proposition (USP)? Conducting market research and understanding the competitive landscape will help you determine if your business idea has the potential to be successful.
- **Feasibility and Profitability:** Can you realistically develop and launch this business concept? Consider the resources you'll need, the costs involved, and your pricing strategy. Will your business generate enough revenue to be profitable in the long run?
- **Scalability and Growth Potential:** Does your business idea have the potential to grow beyond your local market? Can you envision expanding your product offerings or services in the future? Thinking about scalability from the outset can help you develop a business plan that facilitates future growth.

Refining Your Ideas:

The brainstorming process is rarely a one-shot deal. As you evaluate your ideas, you might find yourself refining them, combining elements from different concepts, or even coming up with entirely new ideas. Embrace this iterative process.

Don't be afraid to revisit your initial brainstorming sessions and continue to explore new possibilities.

Remember: The most successful business ideas often address a problem or frustration that others have simply grown accustomed to. By keeping your eyes peeled for unmet needs, challenging the status quo, and unleashing your inner innovator, you can transform a spark of inspiration into a thriving business. The next chapter will delve into the world of market research, equipping you with the tools to assess the viability of your business idea and ensure it resonates with your target market.

CHAPTER 2
PLANNING FOR SUCCESS

SETTING SMART GOALS AND OBJECTIVES

The road to entrepreneurial success is paved with well-defined goals. As a budding teen entrepreneur, setting SMART goals and objectives will be your compass, guiding your actions and keeping you focused on achieving your aspirations.

Understanding SMART Goals:

SMART is an acronym that stands for Specific, Measurable, Achievable, Relevant, and Time-Bound. Each of these elements plays a crucial role in crafting effective goals that propel your business forward.

- **Specific:** Ambiguous goals lack direction and leave room for misinterpretation. A specific goal clearly defines what you want to achieve. For instance, instead of saying "I want to grow my business," a specific goal might be "Increase online sales by 20% within the next quarter."
- **Measurable:** How will you know if you've achieved your goal? Measurable goals include quantifiable elements that allow you to track your progress. In the previous example, the increase in online sales by 20% is a measurable metric.
- **Achievable:** While ambition is admirable, setting unrealistic goals can be demotivating. Your goals should be challenging yet achievable. Consider your resources, skills, and market conditions when setting goals. Perhaps aiming for a 50% increase in online

sales might be unrealistic initially, but a 20% increase might be a more achievable first step.

- **Relevant:** Your goals should be relevant to your overall business objectives and aligned with your long-term vision. Don't get sidetracked by pursuing goals that don't contribute to the success of your business. If your primary goal is to build brand awareness, increasing online sales might be more relevant than focusing solely on social media follower count.
- **Time-Bound:** Assign a specific timeframe for achieving your goals. This creates a sense of urgency and helps you develop a timeline for action. In the example above, the timeframe is "within the next quarter."

Setting SMART Objectives:

Objectives are the specific actions you will take to achieve your goals. They break down your overarching goals into smaller, manageable steps. When creating objectives, ensure they are also SMART:

- **Specific:** Clearly define the actions you will take to reach your goals. Instead of "Improve marketing efforts," a specific objective might be "Launch a targeted social media campaign on Instagram to reach a wider audience of teenagers."
- **Measurable:** Track the progress of your objectives by establishing measurable metrics. For the social media campaign objective, you might track metrics like follower growth, engagement rates, and website traffic generated from the campaign.
- **Achievable:** Be realistic about the resources and time needed to complete your objectives. You might aim to increase your Instagram followers by 10% within a month, a specific and achievable target.

- **Relevant:** Each objective should directly contribute to achieving your broader goals. The social media campaign objective directly aligns with the goal of increasing brand awareness amongst teenagers.
- **Time-Bound:** Set deadlines for completing each objective. This helps you stay on track and ensure timely progress towards your goals.

Developing a SMART Goals and Objectives Framework:

Here's a step-by-step approach to develop a comprehensive framework of SMART goals and objectives for your business:

1. **Brainstorm Your Overall Business Goals:** What do you want to achieve with your business? Do you aim to increase sales, establish brand recognition, or fill a specific gap in the market? Write down your overarching business goals.
2. **Prioritize Your Goals:** Not all goals are created equal. Identify the most critical goals that will have the most significant impact on your business success.
3. **Break Down Each Goal into Objectives:** For each prioritized goal, develop a series of SMART objectives that outline the specific actions you will take to achieve that goal.
4. **Assign Timeframes and Resources:** Allocate realistic deadlines for completing each objective and identify the resources you'll need to achieve them.
5. **Track Your Progress and Adapt:** Regularly monitor your progress towards your goals and objectives. Don't be afraid to adjust your goals or objectives as needed based on market conditions, your learnings, and any unexpected hurdles that arise.

Examples of SMART Goals and Objectives:

Here are some illustrative examples to showcase how to apply the SMART framework to your business:

- **Goal (Specific):** Increase online sales of handmade jewelry by 20% within the next quarter.
- **Objectives (SMART):**
    - **Objective 1:** Launch a targeted social media campaign on Instagram to reach a wider audience of teenagers (Specific). Track the number of new followers and engagement rates on the campaign (Measurable). Allocate 2 hours per week for content creation and posting (Achievable). Align content with the interests of teenage customers (Relevant). Achieve a 10% increase in Instagram followers within the month (Time-Bound).
    - **Objective 2:** Partner with a local influencer who caters to a teenage audience (Specific). Negotiate a product placement or review opportunity (Measurable). Secure a partnership within the next month (Achievable). Increase brand awareness amongst the influencer's followers (Relevant). Finalize the partnership agreement within two weeks (Time-Bound).
    - **Objective 3:** Offer a discount code for online purchases through social media promotions (Specific). Track the number of redemptions using the discount code (Measurable). Allocate a budget for the discount promotion (Achievable). Attract new customers and encourage repeat purchases (Relevant). Implement the discount code promotion within the next week (Time-Bound).

Beyond SMART: Additional Strategies for Goal Setting:

While the SMART framework is a powerful tool, consider these additional strategies to strengthen your goal-setting process:

- **Visualize Your Success:** Take time to visualize achieving your goals. Create a vision board with images and affirmations that represent your aspirations. This can boost your motivation and keep you focused on the long-term vision.
- **Break Down Large Goals into Smaller Milestones:** Large goals can feel overwhelming. Divide them into smaller, achievable milestones to create a sense of accomplishment as you progress.
- **Celebrate Your Wins:** Acknowledge and celebrate your achievements, big or small. Taking the time to celebrate your progress reinforces positive behaviors and keeps you motivated.
- **Develop a Growth Mindset:** Embrace challenges as opportunities to learn and grow. View setbacks as temporary roadblocks on your path to success.
- **Seek Support and Accountability:** Share your goals with trusted friends, mentors, or family members. Having a support system can provide encouragement and hold you accountable for your progress.

Setting SMART goals and objectives is an essential skill for any entrepreneur, but especially for teenagers venturing into the business world. By clearly defining your aspirations, breaking them down into actionable steps, and consistently monitoring progress, you can transform your business dreams into a thriving reality.

CONDUCTING MARKET RESEARCH AND COMPETITOR ANALYSIS

Before you dive headfirst into launching your business, it's crucial to understand the market landscape, identify your target audience, and analyze your competition.

Understanding Market Research:

Market research is the systematic process of gathering information about your target market and the overall industry in which you plan to operate. This information helps you:

- **Validate Your Business Idea:** Does a genuine need or demand exist for your product or service? Market research can help you assess the viability of your idea and identify potential gaps in the market.
- **Identify Your Target Market:** Who are your ideal customers? What are their demographics, needs, preferences, and buying behaviors? Understanding your target market allows you to tailor your marketing strategies and product offerings for maximum impact.
- **Analyze Your Competition:** Who are your competitors? What are their strengths and weaknesses? Market research provides valuable insights into the competitive landscape, helping you differentiate your business and identify opportunities.
- **Develop a Winning Business Plan:** Market research forms the foundation of a well-developed business plan. The information you gather will inform your marketing strategies, financial projections, and overall business goals.

Market Research Techniques:

There are various market research techniques at your disposal, and the most effective approach will depend on your specific business idea and resources. Here are some valuable techniques to consider:

- **Secondary Research:** This involves gathering existing data and information from credible sources. Utilize free resources like government reports, industry publications, and online databases. Explore libraries and educational institutions for relevant market research reports.
- **Surveys:** Create online or paper surveys to gather data directly from your target market. Surveys allow you to collect information about demographics, preferences, and buying habits. Keep your surveys concise and easy to understand, and ensure your questions are relevant to your business idea.
- **Interviews:** Conduct one-on-one interviews with potential customers to gain deeper insights. This allows for more nuanced answers and fosters a more personal connection with your target audience. Prepare thoughtful interview questions beforehand and actively listen to the feedback you receive.
- **Focus Groups:** Gather a small group of potential customers for a moderated discussion about your business idea or product prototype. Focus groups allow for brainstorming and can reveal valuable insights into consumer perceptions. Ensure the participants in your focus group represent your target audience.
- **Observation:** Pay close attention to your surroundings and the behavior of your target market. What are people buying? How do they interact with similar products or services? Observe trends and identify unmet needs based on your observations.

Competitor Analysis

A thorough competitor analysis is an essential component of market research. By understanding your competitors, you can identify opportunities to differentiate your business and gain a competitive edge. Here's what a competitor analysis should entail:

- **Identify Your Competitors:** Who are the businesses directly and indirectly competing with your product or service? Consider online competitors and local businesses catering to the same target market.
- **Analyze Their Strengths and Weaknesses:** Research your competitors' products or services, pricing strategies, marketing tactics, and customer reviews. Identify their strengths that you can learn from and their weaknesses that you can exploit to differentiate your business.
- **Identify Market Gaps:** Are there any areas where your competitors fall short? Perhaps they lack a specific product variation, have limited online presence, or offer poor customer service. These gaps represent opportunities for your business to enter the market and fill the void.

Competitive Analysis Techniques:

Utilize the following techniques to gather valuable information about your competitors:

- **Website Analysis:** Visit your competitors' websites and social media pages. Analyze their content, branding, and messaging. Identify the keywords they use and the target audience they portray.
- **Mystery Shopping:** Pose as a potential customer and visit competitor stores or websites. Evaluate their

customer service standards, sales techniques, and overall customer experience.

- **Industry Reports:** Industry publications and research firms often provide in-depth reports on specific markets and competitor analysis. Utilize these resources to gain valuable insights into the competitive landscape.
- **Competitive Reviews:** Read online reviews from customers who have used your competitors' products or services. Identify recurring themes and areas for improvement that your business can address.

Making Use of Market Research and Competitor Analysis

The information you gather through market research and competitor analysis should inform every aspect of your business plan. Here are some key areas of application:

- **Product Development:** Market research helps you refine your product or service based on customer needs and preferences. Competitor analysis allows you to identify gaps in the market and develop unique features that differentiate your offering.
- **Marketing and Sales Strategies:** Understanding your target market's demographics, buying behaviors, and preferred communication channels allows you to develop targeted marketing campaigns. Analyzing competitor marketing tactics can inspire your own strategies while also revealing opportunities to stand out with unique messaging or promotional offers.
- **Pricing Strategy:** Market research helps you determine the ideal price point for your product or service based on customer perceived value and competitor pricing strategies.
- **Business Location:** For brick-and-mortar businesses, market research can inform your decision

on where to locate your store. Analyze competitor locations and identify areas with high foot traffic and a demographic that aligns with your target market.

- **Financial Projections:** Market research data on industry trends, competitor pricing, and customer demand allows you to develop more realistic and accurate financial projections for your business plan.

Market research and competitor analysis are ongoing processes. As your business evolves and the market landscape changes, it's crucial to stay informed and update your research regularly.

Advanced Market Research Techniques

While the techniques mentioned above provide a solid foundation, there are additional approaches you can explore as your business grows and your resources expand:

- **Social Media Listening:** Utilize social media listening tools to track online conversations about your industry, competitors, and relevant keywords. This allows you to gain deeper insights into customer sentiment and identify emerging trends.
- **A/B Testing:** Conduct A/B testing to compare different versions of your marketing materials, website design, or product features. This data-driven approach allows you to optimize your offerings for maximum impact.
- **Customer Relationship Management (CRM) Systems:** Utilize CRM systems to collect and analyze customer data, including purchase history, preferences, and feedback. This data can be invaluable for developing targeted marketing campaigns and fostering stronger customer relationships.

By conducting thorough market research and competitor analysis, you equip yourself with the knowledge and insights necessary to navigate the ever-changing business landscape. This information empowers you to make informed decisions, tailor your offerings to your target market, and ultimately position your business for long-term success.

CREATING A BUSINESS PLAN

Your entrepreneurial journey takes a monumental leap forward with the creation of a business plan. This comprehensive document serves as your roadmap to success, outlining your business concept, target market, marketing strategies, financial projections, and operational plan. Investors, lenders, and even yourself will utilize this document to assess the viability and potential of your business.

The Purpose and Benefits of a Business Plan:

Beyond securing funding, a business plan offers a multitude of benefits for teen entrepreneurs:

- **Clarity and Focus:** The process of crafting a business plan forces you to crystallize your ideas, identify potential challenges, and develop clear strategies for overcoming them.
- **Communication Tool:** Your business plan serves as a communication tool for potential investors, partners, and even employees. It clearly communicates your vision, goals, and the value proposition of your business.
- **Decision-Making Guide:** As your business evolves, your business plan serves as a reference point for making informed decisions. It outlines your long-term goals and helps you stay aligned with your initial vision.

- **Financial Roadmap:** The financial projections within your business plan guide your financial decision-making. It helps you track your progress, identify areas for improvement, and ensure your business is on track for profitability.

Essential Components of a Winning Business Plan:

A well-structured business plan typically includes the following core components:

- **Executive Summary:** This concise overview serves as a first impression for your reader. It highlights your business concept, target market, competitive advantage, and financial projections. The executive summary should be compelling and pique the reader's interest to delve deeper into your plan.
- **Company Description:** This section provides a detailed description of your business, including its name, legal structure (sole proprietorship, partnership, etc.), mission statement, and the products or services you offer.
- **Market Analysis:** Demonstrate your understanding of the market landscape. Analyze your target market, including demographics, needs, buying behaviors, and any relevant industry trends. Identify your competitors and outline their strengths and weaknesses.
- **Marketing Plan:** Detail your strategies for reaching your target market and promoting your business. This includes your chosen marketing channels (social media, online advertising, partnerships), pricing strategy, and sales plan.
- **Management Team:** If you have partners or team members involved in the business, showcase their qualifications and experience. Highlight the skills and expertise you bring to the table that will contribute to the success of the venture.

- **Operations Plan:** Outline the day-to-day operations of your business. This includes details on your production process, inventory management, customer service protocols, and any necessary permits or licenses.
- **Financial Projections:** This section showcases the financial viability of your business. Include income statements, balance sheets, and cash flow projections. Demonstrate how your business will generate revenue, manage expenses, and achieve profitability.

Crafting Your Business Plan: Step-by-Step Guide

Here's a step-by-step guide to walk you through the process of creating your business plan:

1. **Brainstorm and Research:** Gather your thoughts and conduct thorough market research. Identify your business concept, target market, and competitive landscape.
2. **Develop a Business Model Canvas:** Consider using a Business Model Canvas, a visual tool that helps you map out the core components of your business model, including customer segments, value propositions, channels, and revenue streams.
3. **Write the Executive Summary:** Craft a concise and compelling summary that captures the essence of your business plan.
4. **Flesh Out Each Section:** Utilize the information you gathered to fill in each section of your business plan, following the structure outlined above.
5. **Seek Feedback and Revise:** Share your draft business plan with trusted mentors, family, or friends. Incorporate their feedback and revise your plan accordingly.

Templates and Resources:

To help you get started, there are numerous free and paid business plan templates available online. Utilize these templates as a starting point, but remember to customize them to fit the specifics of your business. Here are some valuable resources to consider:

- **SCORE:** The U.S. Small Business Administration (SBA) offers free business plan templates and resources through SCORE, a network of volunteer mentors who advise small businesses. (https://www.score.org/templates-resources)
- **Bplans:** This website offers a variety of business plan templates and resources specifically tailored for different industries and business types. (https://www.bplans.com/)
- **U.S. Small Business Administration (SBA):** The SBA website provides a wealth of information and resources for aspiring entrepreneurs, including business plan templates and guides. (https://www.sba.gov/)

Tailoring Your Business Plan for Different Business Types

While the core components remain consistent, your business plan might require specific adjustments depending on your business model. Here are some considerations:

- **Product-Based Businesses:** For businesses selling physical products, dedicate a section to product development and sourcing strategies. Outline your production process, quality control measures, and inventory management plan.
- **Service-Based Businesses:** For businesses offering services, emphasize the skills and experience of your

team members. Detail your service offerings, pricing structure, and customer service protocols.

- **Online Businesses:** For e-commerce businesses, delve deeper into your online marketing strategies, website development plans, and fulfillment process. Highlight your cybersecurity measures and data privacy policies.

Remember: There's no one-size-fits-all approach to crafting a business plan. The key is to tailor the document to effectively communicate the unique aspects and potential of your business.

Presenting Your Business Plan with Confidence

Once your business plan is finalized, be prepared to present it with confidence. Here are some tips to ensure a successful presentation:

- **Know Your Audience:** Tailor your presentation to your specific audience, whether it's potential investors, lenders, or business partners.
- **Focus on the Key Points:** Don't overwhelm your audience with excessive detail. Focus on the most important aspects of your business plan and highlight your competitive advantages.
- **Be Passionate and Enthusiastic:** Your enthusiasm for your business will be contagious. Demonstrate your belief in your vision and your commitment to making your business a success.
- **Practice Makes Perfect:** Rehearse your presentation beforehand to ensure clarity, timing, and flow. Be prepared to answer questions and address any potential concerns.

Your business plan is not a static document. As your business evolves and grows, revisit your plan and update it regularly. Reflect on your progress, adapt your strategies based on new information, and ensure your plan continues to accurately represent your thriving business.

CHAPTER 3

FOUNDATIONS FOR YOUR BUSINESS

CHOOSING A LEGAL STRUCTURE

As your business transforms from a promising idea into a tangible reality, one of your crucial decisions involves selecting the appropriate legal structure. This framework determines how your business operates, your tax obligations, and your personal liability. This chapter equips you with a comprehensive understanding of the most common legal structures for businesses, empowering you to make an informed decision that best suits your needs.

Understanding Legal Structures

A legal structure defines the formal organization of your business and establishes the relationship between the business and its owners. The primary legal structures for businesses include:

- **Sole Proprietorship:** This is the simplest and most common legal structure for teen entrepreneurs. In a sole proprietorship, you are the sole owner and operator of the business. There is no legal distinction between you and your business; all profits and losses flow directly through your personal tax return.
- **Partnership:** A partnership involves two or more people co-owning and managing a business. Partners share profits, losses, and management responsibilities according to the terms outlined in a partnership agreement. A written partnership agreement is highly recommended to avoid potential disputes and clearly define each partner's roles, responsibilities, and profit-sharing arrangements.

- **Limited Liability Company (LLC):** An LLC offers a balance between the simplicity of a sole proprietorship and the liability protection of a corporation. LLCs offer limited liability protection, meaning the owners' personal assets are shielded from business debts and lawsuits, up to a point. Profits and losses pass through to the owners' personal tax returns.
- **Corporation:** Corporations are complex legal structures typically associated with larger businesses. They involve a separate legal entity from the owners, with its own board of directors and officers. Corporations offer the strongest liability protection but also come with more complex regulations and reporting requirements.

Choosing the Right Structure for Your Business:

The ideal legal structure for your business depends on several factors. Here are key considerations to guide your decision:

- **Liability Protection:** How important is it for you to shield your personal assets from business liabilities? Sole proprietorships offer no liability protection, while LLCs and corporations provide a layer of separation.
- **Number of Owners:** If you plan to operate your business solo, a sole proprietorship might suffice. If you have partners, a partnership or LLC is more appropriate.
- **Tax Considerations:** Sole proprietorships and partnerships are considered "pass-through entities." Profits and losses pass through to the owners' personal tax returns. Corporations pay income tax on their profits before distributing dividends to shareholders, which can result in double taxation.
- **Complexity and Regulations:** Sole proprietorships are the least complex structure, while corporations

have the most stringent regulations and reporting requirements. LLCs offer a middle ground.

- **Future Growth Potential:** If you envision significant future growth for your business, a corporation might be a better choice due to its scalability and ability to attract investors.

Benefits and Drawbacks of Each Structure:

Here's a breakdown of the key advantages and disadvantages of each legal structure to aid your decision-making process:

- **Sole Proprietorship:**
  - **Benefits:** Easy to set up and manage, low cost, all profits belong to you.
  - **Drawbacks:** No liability protection, limited access to funding, business ceases to exist when you do.
- **Partnership:**
  - **Benefits:** Shared workload and expertise, potential for increased investment and resources.
  - **Drawbacks:** Unlimited liability for all partners, potential for disagreements, complex profit-sharing arrangements.
- **Limited Liability Company (LLC):**
  - **Benefits:** Pass-through taxation, limited liability protection, relatively simple to form and maintain.
  - **Drawbacks:** May have filing fees and annual reporting requirements, not ideal for attracting large-scale investment.

- **Corporation:**
    - **Benefits:** Strongest liability protection, ability to raise capital through stock issuance, potential for perpetual existence.
    - **Drawbacks:** Most complex and expensive structure to set up and maintain, double taxation, extensive regulations and reporting requirements.

Additional Considerations for Teen Entrepreneurs:

As a minor, there might be additional legal considerations specific to your situation. In some cases, you might require parental consent or involvement in establishing your chosen legal structure. It's crucial to consult with a legal professional familiar with business law and the specific regulations in your area.

Seeking Professional Guidance:

Choosing the right legal structure is a critical decision that can have long-term implications for your business. Consider seeking guidance from a qualified business attorney or accountant who can assess your specific needs and recommend the most suitable structure for your business.

The legal structure you choose serves as the foundation upon which your business will grow. By carefully considering the factors outlined above and seeking professional guidance if needed, you can make an informed decision that ensures your business operates efficiently, protects your personal assets, and paves the way for long-term success.

Considerations for Specific Business Models

While the core legal structures apply to most businesses, there might be specific considerations depending on your chosen business model:

- **Home-Based Businesses:** If you operate your business from home, zoning regulations might influence your choice of legal structure. Some towns or cities might have restrictions on home-based businesses operated as corporations.
- **Online Businesses:** If your business operates solely online, you might have more flexibility in choosing a legal structure as location might not be a major factor. However, if you plan to sell digital products or services internationally, consult with an attorney to ensure compliance with relevant tax and regulatory requirements.
- **Businesses with Intellectual Property:** If your business involves intellectual property such as trademarks or copyrights, forming an LLC or corporation might offer additional protection for your assets.

Legal structures are not permanent choices. As your business evolves, you might consider changing your legal structure to better suit your changing needs. Always consult with a legal professional before making any significant changes to your business structure.

Choosing the right legal structure is a crucial step in establishing a strong foundation for your business. By understanding your options, seeking professional guidance, and making an informed decision, you empower your business to thrive and achieve its full potential.

OBTAINING NECESSARY PERMITS AND LICENSES

The entrepreneurial journey for a teenager can be exhilarating, but navigating the permit maze can feel like a confusing detour. Before you open your doors (physical or virtual), understanding the specific requirements in your area is crucial to ensure legal and compliant operations.

Why Permits and Licenses Matter

Obtaining the necessary permits and licenses goes beyond simply checking a box. It's about safeguarding yourself, your customers, and your burgeoning business empire. Here's a breakdown of why securing the right permits and licenses is essential:

- **Legality and Avoiding Penalties:** Operating without the required permits and licenses is a recipe for trouble. Fines, penalties, or even forced closure can derail your entrepreneurial dreams. Don't let a simple oversight become a major setback.
- **Protecting Your Customers:** Certain permits and licenses ensure you adhere to safety and health regulations. For example, a food-service business with a health department permit demonstrates a commitment to proper food handling, protecting your customers from potential health hazards.
- **Building Business Credibility:** Having the necessary permits and licenses signifies professionalism and compliance. This fosters trust with your customers and potential partners, giving your business a competitive edge.
- **Unlocking Valuable Resources:** The permitting process can connect you with valuable resources. Many local government agencies offering permits also provide support and guidance for new businesses. This

can be a goldmine of information and assistance for a teen entrepreneur.

Understanding the Landscape

The specific permits and licenses you need depend on a complex interplay of factors:

- **Your Business Location:** Local and state regulations determine the required permits and licenses. Operating in a bustling city might require additional permits compared to a rural area. Researching your specific location is crucial.
- **Your Business Model:** The type of business you operate dictates your permit needs. A bakery will have different requirements compared to a graphic design service. Understanding your business model is the first step to identifying the necessary permits.
- **Your Business Activities:** The specific activities your business engages in might trigger the need for additional permits. For example, selling handcrafted jewelry at a farmers market might require a vendor permit, while offering dog-walking services might require a business license and potentially a pet care license depending on local regulations.

Common Permits and Licenses for Businesses:

While the specific requirements will vary, here's a breakdown of some of the most common permits and licenses relevant to businesses:

- **Business License:** This fundamental permit allows you to operate your business within a specific jurisdiction. Issued by your local government office, it allows you to conduct business and collect sales tax if applicable. Consider this the "passport" to launching your business legally.

- **Home Occupation Permit:** If you operate your business from the comfort of your own home, a home occupation permit might be necessary. This ensures your home-based business complies with zoning regulations and doesn't disrupt the neighborhood. Turning your bedroom into a design studio? Check with your local zoning board for home occupation permit requirements.
- **Sales Tax Permit:** If you're selling tangible goods or specific services (like car washes or pet grooming), you might need a sales tax permit. This authorizes you to collect and remit sales tax to the government. Understanding your sales tax obligations is crucial to avoid any tax-related issues down the road.
- **Health Department Permit:** Businesses involved in food preparation, body art (like piercings or tattoos), or other activities regulated by health codes require a permit from the local health department. This ensures your business adheres to sanitation and safety standards, protecting both your customers and your reputation.
- **Fire Marshal Permit:** Depending on your business type and location, you might need a fire marshal permit. This ensures your business meets fire safety regulations, including proper fire extinguisher placement and escape routes. Always prioritize safety; a fire marshal permit demonstrates your commitment to a safe environment for your customers and employees (if applicable).

Permits and Licenses for Specialized Businesses

The business world is diverse, and so are the permits and licenses required. Here's a closer look at some specific business models:

- **Online Businesses:** Even if you operate solely online, you might still need to comply with sales tax regulations in your state and potentially other states where you have customers. Research economic nexus laws to determine your sales tax obligations. Don't let your virtual storefront become a tax haven; understanding economic nexus is crucial for online businesses.

- **Event-Based Businesses:** Businesses that participate in fairs, farmers markets, or other temporary events might require vendor permits from the event organizers. These permits often come with specific requirements related to booth setup, product display, and safety regulations. Ensure you understand the organizer's permit requirements before booking your spot at the next craft fair.
- **Service-Based Businesses:** Certain service-based businesses, such as those offering pet grooming or computer repair, might require professional licenses depending on the service offered. Research any licensing requirements specific to your chosen service industry. Don't provide pet grooming services without the proper licenses; ensuring you meet professional licensing standards builds trust with your customers.
- **Businesses with Employees:** If you plan to hire employees, even part-time help, you'll need to register your business with the federal government to obtain an Employer Identification Number (EIN). This number is used for tax purposes and employee payroll. Hiring a friend to help you with your online business? An EIN ensures you're compliant with federal tax regulations.

Finding the Right Information

The best place to start your research is your local government office's website or by contacting the relevant department directly. Many government websites offer user-friendly permit and license search tools that allow you to identify the specific requirements for your business type and location. Think of these websites as your roadmap to navigating the permitting maze.

Here are some additional resources to help you on your entrepreneurial journey:

- **U.S. Small Business Administration (SBA):** The SBA website provides a wealth of information on business permits and licenses, including links to state and local resources. This government agency is a treasure trove of information for aspiring teen entrepreneurs. (https://www.sba.gov/)
- **SCORE:** SCORE, a network of volunteer mentors offered through the SBA, can connect you with experienced business professionals who can offer guidance on permits and licenses specific to your area. Consider SCORE mentors as your personal guides through the permitting process. (https://www.score.org/)
- **Business Associations:** Industry-specific associations often provide resources and guidance on permits and regulations relevant to your business type. These associations can be a valuable source of information tailored to your specific industry.

Tips for Obtaining Permits and Licenses

- **Start Early:** The permitting process can take time, so begin researching and applying for permits well in advance of your launch date. Don't wait until the last minute to navigate the permitting maze.

- **Be Organized:** Gather all the necessary documentation and information required for each permit application. This might include your business plan, proof of ownership or lease agreement for your business location, tax identification numbers, and any other documents specified by the issuing agency. Organization is key to a smooth permitting process.
- **Ask Questions:** Don't hesitate to ask questions of government officials or permit specialists if anything is unclear. There are no silly questions when it comes to ensuring your business is compliant. Seek clarification if you're unsure about any aspect of the permitting process.
- **Maintain Records:** Keep copies of all your permits and licenses for your records. These documents will be vital during inspections or renewals. Having a well-organized filing system for your permits and licenses ensures you're always prepared.

Obtaining the necessary permits and licenses demonstrates your commitment to operating a responsible and compliant business. By taking the time to understand the requirements and navigate the permitting process, you ensure your business operates legally, protects your customers, and fosters a strong foundation for long-term success. Remember that compliance isn't a burden; it's your superpower, empowering you to build a thriving business venture.

FUNDING YOUR BUSINESS VENTURE

The road to financial self-sufficiency through your business starts with a critical first step: securing the resources to launch and grow your venture. In this section, we will be providing you with a comprehensive understanding of various funding options, empowering you to choose the approach that best aligns with your business goals and financial situation.

Understanding Your Funding Needs

Before diving into the world of financing, it's crucial to assess your specific needs. Consider the following factors:

- **Startup Costs:** This goes beyond the basic equipment and supplies. Identify the initial expenses required to launch your business, such as:
    - **Equipment:** Do you need specialized tools, machinery, or software to operate?
    - **Inventory:** For product-based businesses, factor in the cost of raw materials, finished products, and potentially packaging.
    - **Marketing Materials:** Will you need business cards, flyers, website development, or social media advertising?
    - **Permits and Licenses:** Research any necessary permits or licenses required to operate legally in your location. Factor in application fees and potential ongoing renewal costs.
    - **Location:** If your business has a physical presence, consider rent, utilities, and any necessary renovations to your workspace.
- **Operational Costs:** Estimate ongoing expenses that will keep your business running, such as:
    - **Rent and Utilities:** For a physical location, factor in monthly rent, electricity, water, and internet costs.
    - **Supplies:** Consider ongoing needs for office supplies, cleaning products, raw materials (for product-based businesses), or software subscriptions.

  - **Marketing and Advertising:** Budget for ongoing marketing efforts to maintain customer reach and brand awareness.
  - **Professional Services:** Depending on your business model, you might need ongoing expenses for legal services, accounting, or web maintenance.
  - **Payroll:** If you plan to hire employees, factor in salary or hourly wages, payroll taxes, and employee benefits (if offered).
- **Growth Plans:** Don't just focus on the present; consider any potential future expenses related to scaling your business, such as:
  - **Expanding Product Line:** If you plan to offer new products or services, factor in research and development, marketing for new offerings, and potential inventory costs for new products.
  - **Entering New Markets:** Scaling your business geographically might require additional marketing efforts, travel expenses, or establishing a physical presence in a new location.
  - **Hiring Additional Staff:** As your business grows, so might your staffing needs. Consider future costs associated with hiring new employees.

BOOTSTRAPPING

Bootstrapping is a popular funding approach for teen entrepreneurs, relying on personal savings, sweat equity (your time and effort), and resourceful creativity. Bootstrapped businesses are self-funded and operate with minimal external investment.

Benefits of Bootstrapping:

- **Maintains Control:** You retain full ownership and decision-making power over your business. This allows you to make strategic choices without the influence of investors.
- **Teaches Valuable Lessons:** Bootstrapping fosters resourcefulness, financial discipline, and a deep understanding of your business's financial health. You learn to make the most of every resource and become a savvy business owner.
- **Low Barrier to Entry:** You can launch your business without complex loan applications or investor pitches. This allows you to get started quickly and test your business concept in the real world.

Challenges of Bootstrapping:

- **Limited Capital:** Bootstrapping might restrict your ability to invest in significant resources or rapid growth. This can limit your initial marketing reach or ability to scale quickly.
- **Time Constraints:** Balancing school, work, and running a bootstrapped business can be demanding. Time management skills are crucial to juggle all your responsibilities.
- **Marketing Limitations:** Bootstrapped businesses might have limited funds for extensive marketing campaigns. Reaching a wider audience and building brand awareness can be challenging on a tight budget.

Creative Bootstrapping Strategies

- **Pre-Selling:** Consider pre-selling your product or service to generate initial capital before launch. This can be a great way to validate demand for your offering and secure early funding. Offer discounts or early-bird specials to incentivize pre-orders.

- **Bartering:** Explore bartering opportunities for services or resources you need in exchange for your own skills or products. This could involve trading web design services for marketing help or offering handmade crafts in exchange for website development.
- **Crowdfunding:** Platforms like Kickstarter or Indiegogo allow you to raise funds from a large pool of online contributors. Present your business idea in a compelling way, highlighting the benefits of your product or service and offering tiered rewards for different contribution levels. This can be a fantastic way to test the market, generate interest, and raise capital simultaneously.

- **Freelancing or Side Hustles:** Utilize your skills and free time to earn additional income specifically for your business venture. Freelance writing, graphic design, pet sitting, or tutoring services are just a few possibilities.
- **Resourceful Marketing:** Explore low-cost or free marketing strategies to reach your target audience. Utilize social media platforms organically, participate in local markets or community events, partner with other businesses for cross-promotion, or create informative blog content to establish yourself as an expert.
- **Grants and Competitions:** Research opportunities for grants or competitions specifically targeted towards young entrepreneurs. These can offer financial rewards or valuable resources to jumpstart your business.

SAVINGS

Saving a portion of your income allows you to build a financial cushion to launch your business. Earning money through part-time jobs, allowances, or side hustles can contribute to your business funding.

Benefits of Funding with Savings:

- **Reduced Risk:** Using your own savings minimizes financial risk by avoiding debt or dependence on external investors. You maintain control over your finances and aren't obligated to repay loans with interest.
- **Sense of Ownership:** Investing your own money builds a strong sense of ownership and commitment to your business. You'll be highly motivated to see your hard-earned savings turn into a successful venture.
- **Flexibility:** You can use your savings without the restrictions or repayment terms associated with loans or investments. This allows for greater flexibility in allocating funds to different areas of your business.

Challenges of Funding with Savings:

- **Limited Capital:** Individual savings might not be sufficient for businesses requiring significant initial investment. Especially for high-cost inventory or equipment needs, relying solely on savings might limit your startup options.
- **Delayed Gratification:** Saving requires delaying purchases or experiences, demanding financial discipline. It might take time to accumulate enough savings to launch your business idea.
- **Time Investment:** Building up enough savings might take longer than other funding options, potentially delaying your business launch. However, the benefits of reduced risk and ownership can make the wait worthwhile.

FAMILY AND FRIENDS

Family and friends can be a valuable source of financial support. If you choose to seek funding from loved ones, communicate your business plan clearly and establish realistic expectations regarding repayment or potential returns. Formalize any agreements with a written loan contract outlining terms and conditions.

Benefits of Funding from Family and Friends:

- **Potential Flexibility:** Family and friends might be more flexible with repayment terms compared to traditional lenders. They might be understanding of potential delays or offer lower interest rates on loans.
- **Emotional Support:** Financial support from loved ones can be accompanied by valuable encouragement and practical advice. Their belief in your idea can be a motivating force.
- **Early Investment:** Family and friends might be willing to invest early in your business idea, helping you get off the ground before you have a proven track record for traditional lenders.

Challenges of Funding from Family and Friends:

- **Mixing Business and Personal Relationships:** Financial issues can strain personal relationships. Ensure clear communication and establish professional agreements to avoid misunderstandings.
- **Limited Capital:** The amount of funding available from family and friends might be limited. Don't rely solely on loved ones for substantial funding needs.
- **Pressure to Succeed:** Feeling obligated to succeed due to personal investment can be stressful. Manage expectations and prioritize open communication with your family and friends.

Loans: Leveraging External Capital

Business loans can provide the necessary capital to launch or grow your business. Carefully evaluate different loan options and understand the associated interest rates, repayment terms, and potential risks. Only borrow what you can realistically repay based on your projected business income.

Types of Loans for Businesses:

- **Personal Loans:** These unsecured loans typically come with higher interest rates but might be an option if you have good credit (co-signing from a parent or guardian might be required). Use personal loans cautiously, as high-interest rates can strain your business finances.
- **Student Loans:** While not always ideal, some student loan programs allow funds to be used for business purposes under specific conditions. Thorough research and consultation with a financial advisor is crucial before considering this option. Student loans are intended for educational expenses and come with strict repayment terms.
- **Microloans:** These small loans, typically offered by specialized non-profit organizations, can be a good option for teen entrepreneurs. Microloans often come with lower interest rates and mentorship programs to support young business owners.

- **Small Business Administration (SBA) Loans:** The U.S. Small Business Administration (SBA) offers various loan programs specifically designed for small businesses. These loans typically require a strong business plan and good credit but can provide access to significant funding for your venture. Research SBA loan programs like the 7(a) loan or the Microloan program to see if they align with your needs.

Alternative Financing Options

Beyond traditional loans, consider alternative financing options that might be suitable for your business:

- **Angel Investors:** Angel investors are wealthy individuals who invest in early-stage companies with high growth potential. While securing angel investment can be challenging, it can provide significant funding and valuable mentorship for your business. Focus on a well-developed business plan and a clear understanding of your target market to attract angel investors.
- **Venture Capital:** Venture capital firms invest in high-growth startups with the potential for substantial returns. Securing venture capital is highly competitive and typically requires a more established business with a proven track record. This option might not be suitable for most businesses in the early stages.
- **Equipment Leasing:** Leasing equipment allows you to acquire necessary machinery or technology without a large upfront investment. This can be a good option for businesses that rely on specific equipment but might not have the capital to purchase it outright. Leasing comes with ongoing payments, so carefully evaluate the cost-effectiveness compared to purchasing.
- **Invoice Factoring:** This financing option allows you to sell your outstanding invoices to a factoring company at a discount. This can provide immediate access to working capital, but factoring fees can be high. Consider invoice factoring only if your business has a reliable customer base and consistent invoices.

Choosing the Right Funding Option

The ideal funding option for your business depends on several factors:

- **Stage of Development:** Are you just starting out or looking to expand an existing business? Bootstrapping or savings might be suitable for early stages, while loans or angel investors might be more relevant for growth.
- **Funding Needs:** How much capital do you require to launch or grow your business? Consider your specific needs and choose a financing option that provides sufficient resources.
- **Risk Tolerance:** Are you comfortable with the potential debt associated with loans? Bootstrapping or using savings minimizes financial risk but might limit your growth potential.
- **Business Model:** Some financing options might be more suitable for specific business models. For example, equipment leasing might be ideal for businesses reliant on specialized equipment.

Carefully consider the various funding options available and choose the approach that best aligns with your business goals and financial situation. Remember that a successful funding strategy involves not just securing capital but also managing your finances responsibly.

CHAPTER 4
BUILDING YOUR BRAND IDENTITY

CRAFTING A CATCHY BUSINESS NAME

Your business name is more than just words on a sign; it's the first impression you make on potential customers. It's the foundation of your brand identity, shaping how people perceive your venture.

Brainstorming Like a Boss

The journey to a stellar business name begins with a brainstorming session. Gather your supplies – a notebook, pen, and a healthy dose of creativity – and unleash your inner wordsmith. Here are some brainstorming techniques to get you started:

- **Keyword Focus:** Identify keywords that capture the essence of your business. These could be product or service related, or keywords that reflect your brand values. For example, if you sell handmade jewelry, keywords might include "jewelry," "handmade," or "unique." If you offer dog walking services, keywords could be "dog," "walking," "care," or "reliable." Write down a list of relevant keywords to kickstart your brainstorming.
- **Thesaurus Time:** Dust off that trusty thesaurus. Using synonyms for your chosen keywords can spark new ideas and help you discover unique word combinations. For example, instead of simply "jewelry," explore synonyms like "adornment," "embellishment," or "treasure." This can lead to name options you might not have considered otherwise.

- **Descriptive Power:** Consider descriptive words that evoke a feeling or experience related to your business. Think about the emotions you want your brand to evoke – joy, creativity, trust, or value. For example, "Joyful Creations" for a craft business or "Reliable Rovers" for dog walking services.
- **Rhyme and Rhythm:** Catchy names often incorporate rhyme or rhythm, making them easier to remember. Think of iconic brand names like Kit Kat or Coca-Cola. While not essential, rhyming or rhythmic elements can add a touch of memorability to your chosen name.
- **Wordplay and Puns:** If it aligns with your brand image, consider incorporating wordplay or puns into your business name. This can be a fun way to grab attention and showcase your brand personality. For example, "Pawsome Pups" for dog walking services or "Crafty Cat Creations" for a handmade craft business (assuming your target market appreciates cat puns.).
- **Personal Touches (Optional):** For some businesses, incorporating a personal touch can be effective. This could be your own name (think Martha Stewart) or a name with a special meaning related to your business origin story. However, this approach might not be suitable for all businesses, so weigh the pros and cons before using a personal name.

Refining Your Choices

Once you have a list of potential names, it's time to refine your choices. Here are some crucial factors to consider:

- **Availability:** The most brilliant name falls flat if it's already trademarked or in use by another business. Conduct a thorough internet search and trademark check to ensure your chosen name is available.

- **Target Audience Appeal:** Does your name resonate with your target audience? Consider the age group, interests, and preferences of your ideal customer. A name that appeals to children might not be suitable for a business targeting adults.
- **Pronunciation and Spelling:** Choose a name that is easy to pronounce and spell. Avoid overly complex names or words with unusual spellings that could lead to customer confusion.
- **Memorable Magic:** The best business names are memorable. Can people easily recall your name after hearing it once or twice? Aim for a name that sticks in their minds and leaves a lasting impression.
- **Scalability:** Consider the long-term vision for your business. Does the name have room to grow with your venture? Avoid names that are too specific to a single product or service, as you might expand your offerings in the future.
- **Brand Image:** Your business name should reflect the overall image you want to portray. Does it convey professionalism, creativity, fun, or trustworthiness, depending on your brand values?

Shortlisting and Testing

Once you've narrowed down your options to a few strong contenders, it's time to test the waters. Here are some ways to get feedback on your shortlisted names:

- **Get Feedback from Friends and Family:** Ask your friends and family for their honest opinions on your shortlisted names. Gather their thoughts on memorability, pronunciation, and overall impression.
- **Target Audience Feedback (Optional):** If possible, consider getting feedback from your target audience. This could involve online surveys or focus groups with potential customers within your target age

range. Their insights can be invaluable in choosing a name that resonates with your ideal market.

- **Domain Name Availability:** While not the final step, check the availability of domain names corresponding to your shortlisted business names. Securing a domain name that matches your business name creates a seamless online presence for your venture.

Crafting the perfect business name takes time, creativity, and careful consideration. By following these steps and leveraging the brainstorming techniques outlined in this chapter, you'll be well on your way to selecting a catchy and memorable name that captures the essence of your business. Your business name is a cornerstone of your brand identity, so choose wisely and with a vision for future growth.

DESIGNING A LOGO AND VISUAL IDENTITY

Your business name is the foundation, but your visual identity – the logo, colors, fonts, and overall aesthetic – is the face of your brand. It's the visual language that speaks to your target audience, conveying your brand personality and values.

Understanding Your Brand Identity

Before diving into logo creation, take a step back and solidify your brand identity. This is the essence of your business, encompassing your brand values, target audience, and overall message. Ask yourself these key questions:

- **Brand Values:** What are the core values your business represents? Is it creativity, reliability, sustainability, or something else entirely? Identifying your values helps guide your design choices.

- **Target Audience:** Who are you trying to reach with your business? Understanding their age group, interests, and preferences is crucial for creating a visual identity that resonates with them.
- **Brand Personality:** What kind of personality do you want your brand to convey? Fun and playful, professional and sophisticated, or something in between? This personality will be reflected in your visual elements.

Logo Design

Your logo is the visual cornerstone of your brand identity. It's the image that people will associate with your business, so it needs to be memorable, impactful, and communicate your brand essence effectively. Here are some key principles to guide your logo design:

- **Simplicity is Key:** Avoid overly complex designs or an abundance of colors. Simple, clean logos are easier to remember and reproduce across different mediums (online, print, merchandise). Think of iconic logos like Apple's apple or Nike's swoosh.
- **Meaningful Symbolism:** Consider incorporating symbols or icons that subtly represent your brand or product. For example, a paw print for a pet-related business or a paintbrush for an art supply store. However, avoid overly literal symbols that might be unclear to your audience.
- **Color Psychology:** Colors evoke emotions and have specific associations. Research color psychology and choose colors that align with your brand values and target audience. For example, blue is often associated with trust and professionalism, while green evokes feelings of nature and growth.
- **Font Matters:** Choose a font style that reflects your brand personality. Serif fonts convey a sense of

tradition and elegance, while sans-serif fonts are more modern and minimalist. Experiment with different fonts to find one that complements your overall design.

- **Versatility is Crucial:** Your logo needs to be versatile enough to work across different applications, from your website and social media profiles to business cards and printed materials. Ensure it looks good when scaled up or down and translates well into different formats.

DIY Design or Design Help? Exploring Your Options

Creating a logo can be a fun and creative process. Here are some options to consider:

- **DIY Design Tools:** Several free or paid online design tools like Canva or Logo Maker allow you to create your own logo using templates and design elements. This is a good option for budget-conscious entrepreneurs who enjoy getting creative.
- **Freelance Graphic Designers:** Consider hiring a freelance graphic designer with experience in logo design. They can translate your vision into a professional and impactful logo. Freelance platforms like Upwork or Fiverr can help you connect with talented designers.
- **Design Contests:** Some websites host logo design contests where you can present your brand identity and have designers submit logo concepts. This can be a cost-effective way to get a variety of logo options, but the quality can vary depending on the contest platform.

Beyond the Logo

Your logo is the starting point, but your visual identity extends beyond it. Here's how to create a cohesive visual experience for your brand:

- **Color Palette:** Establish a consistent color palette that complements your logo and reflects your brand values. Use this color palette throughout your website, social media, marketing materials, and even packaging (if applicable).
- **Fonts:** Choose a primary font for headlines and a secondary font for body text. Maintain consistency in font usage across different platforms.
- **Imagery:** Use high-quality images that are relevant to your brand and target audience. This could include product photos, lifestyle images, or illustrations that support your brand message.
- **Design Consistency:** Maintain a consistent visual style across all your touchpoints. This builds brand recognition and creates a professional image for your business.

Tools and Resources for Design Success

Here are some handy tools and resources to help you create a stellar visual identity for your business:

- **Free Online Design Tools:** Canva, Adobe Spark, and Stencil offer user-friendly templates and design elements to create social media graphics, presentations, and marketing materials that align with your brand identity. These tools are perfect for beginners or those on a tight budget.
- **Stock Photo and Video Websites:** Websites like Unsplash, Pexels, and Shutterstock offer a vast library of free and paid stock photos and videos that can elevate your visual content. Choose images that are high-quality and resonate with your target audience.
- **Design Inspiration Websites:** Websites like Behance, Dribble, and Pinterest showcase the work of talented graphic designers. Browse these platforms for

creative inspiration and to see how other businesses use visual elements to represent their brands.

The Power of Storytelling

Your visual identity is more than just aesthetics; it's a storytelling tool. Use your logo, colors, fonts, and imagery to tell the story of your brand. What are you passionate about? What problem are you solving for your customers? Weaving a narrative through your visuals creates a deeper connection with your target audience.

Maintaining Your Visual Identity Over Time

Once you've established your visual identity, ensure consistency is your middle name. Use your logo, color palette, and fonts consistently across all your platforms and marketing materials. This reinforces brand recognition and builds trust with your audience. As your business grows, consider evolving your visual identity to maintain a fresh and relevant look, while still retaining core elements that establish brand recognition.

Designing a logo and crafting a compelling visual identity is an exciting step in building your business. By understanding your brand essence, leveraging design tools and resources, and telling a visual story, you can create a unique and impactful presence that resonates with your target audience.

ESTABLISHING YOUR BRAND VOICE AND ONLINE PRESENCE

In today's digital landscape, your online presence is more than just a website; it's the beating heart of your business. It's the platform where you connect with potential customers, tell your brand story, showcase your unique offerings, and build a loyal following.

The Power of Brand Voice

Imagine your brand voice as the soundtrack to your business. It's the personality behind your logo, the tone in your social media captions, and the language used in your product descriptions. A strong brand voice isn't just about aesthetics; it's a strategic tool that fosters trust, builds relationships, and makes your business stand out from the crowd. Here's how a compelling brand voice benefits your teen venture:

- **Customer Connection:** A relatable brand voice allows you to connect with your target audience on a deeper level. It creates a sense of familiarity and makes your business feel approachable – essential for building trust with younger consumers.
- **Memorable Impact:** A distinct brand voice sets you apart from competitors. It becomes instantly recognizable, leaving a lasting impression on potential customers who encounter your content online.
- **Emotional Engagement:** The right tone can evoke emotions in your audience, whether it's excitement about your new product launch, inspiration from your entrepreneurial journey, or amusement from your witty social media posts.
- **Community Building:** A strong brand voice fosters a sense of community around your business. Customers who resonate with your personality and values are more likely to engage with your content, participate in discussions, and become brand advocates.

Understanding Your Audience

Before crafting your brand voice, take a step back and get to know your ideal customer like a close friend. Here are some key questions to consider:

- **Demographics:** What is the age group, gender, and location of your target audience? Understanding their basic demographics helps tailor your communication style to resonate with their specific needs and interests.
- **Online Habits:** Where do they hang out online? Are they avid TikTok users, frequent Instagram scrollers, or Twitter newsfeed enthusiasts? Knowing their preferred platforms allows you to focus your content creation efforts where they'll be seen the most.
- **Interests and Passions:** What are their hobbies, what ignites their curiosity, and what kind of content do they consume online? Knowing their interests allows you to create content that aligns with their passions, sparking their attention and fostering engagement.
- **Challenges and Aspirations:** What problems are you solving for your customers? What are their hopes, dreams, and aspirations? Understanding their challenges allows you to position your brand as a solution and connect with their desire for self-expression, independence, or achieving specific goals.

Developing Your Brand Voice

Once you have a clear picture of your ideal customer, you can begin crafting your brand voice. This symphony of tone and style will guide your communication across all platforms, ensuring consistency and a clear understanding of your brand personality.

- **Tone:** This refers to the emotional feel you want to convey in your communication. Here are some tone options to consider, keeping your target audience in mind:
    - **Friendly and Conversational:** Imagine you're chatting with a friend, using informal language and relatable humor. This tone works well for businesses targeting younger audiences who value authenticity and connection.
    - **Informative and Educational:** This tone positions you as an expert, providing valuable knowledge and insights related to your industry. It's ideal for businesses offering educational products or services.
    - **Motivational and Empowering:** This tone inspires your audience and encourages them to take action. It's effective for businesses that promote self-improvement, creativity, or personal growth.
    - **Playful and Quirky:** This tone injects humor and lightheartedness into your communication, making your brand stand out with a unique personality. It's a good fit for businesses offering fun and creative products or services.
- **Style:** This encompasses the way you use language to express your brand personality. Consider the following:
    - **Sentence Structure:** Do you prefer short and punchy sentences for a fast-paced feel, or longer, descriptive sentences to paint a vivid picture?
    - **Formality Level:** Will you use slang and emojis to connect with a younger audience, or maintain a more formal approach for a professional image?
    - **Word Choice:** Consider the vocabulary that aligns with your brand values. For example, a

sustainable clothing brand might use words like "eco-conscious" and "organic," while a tech startup might favor terms like "cutting-edge" and "innovative."

Crafting Your Brand Voice Statement

Developing a brand voice statement is like creating a mission statement for your communication style. It's a concise document that captures the essence of your brand personality and serves as a guiding light for you and anyone creating content for your business. Here's how to craft your brand voice statement:

- **Start with Your Values:** List your core brand values. For example, if you value creativity and inclusivity, your brand voice might be expressive and welcoming.
- **Consider Your Audience:** Think about the language and tone that would resonate with your target customers. Imagine you're having a conversation with them – how would you speak?
- **Define Your Personality:** Do you want to be seen as playful, informative, or helpful? Identify the personality traits you want your brand voice to embody.
- **Craft a Concise Statement:** Put it all together in a short, impactful statement that captures the essence of your brand voice. For example, "Our brand voice is empowering and supportive, providing teens with the tools and resources to turn their entrepreneurial dreams into reality, all with a sprinkle of humor and a dash of relatability."

Building Your Online Presence

Now that you have a strong brand voice, it's time to establish your online presence – the digital storefront for your business. Here are the key steps involved:

- **Develop a User-Friendly Website:** Your website is your digital headquarters, showcasing your products or services, telling your brand story, and providing a platform for customer interaction. Start with a beginner-friendly website builder like Wix or Squarespace, ensuring your website is mobile-optimized for easy access on smartphones.
    - **Essential Website Elements:** Include clear product descriptions, high-quality photos or videos, testimonials from satisfied customers, and a call to action (CTA) prompting visitors to take the next step, whether it's making a purchase, subscribing to your newsletter, or contacting you for more information.
- **Embrace Social Media Platforms:** Choose the social media platforms where your target audience spends their time. Create engaging content that reflects your brand voice and values, using high-quality visuals, informative captions, and interactive elements like polls and quizzes to encourage audience participation. Here are some platform-specific tips:
    - **Instagram:** Focus on visually appealing content showcasing your products or services in action. Leverage Instagram Stories and Reels to share behind-the-scenes glimpses, product tutorials, or customer testimonials.
    - **TikTok:** Embrace short-form video content that is fun, creative, and informative. Utilize trending sounds, challenges, and transitions to capture attention and showcase your brand personality.

  - **Twitter:** Engage in conversations, share industry news, and provide customer support through quick tweets. Run Twitter polls to gather audience insights and gauge interest in new products or services.
  - **Facebook:** Create a community around your brand, share longer-form content like blog posts or articles, and run targeted ads to reach a wider audience. Utilize Facebook groups to foster discussions among your customers and brand advocates.
- **Content is King:** Consistently create engaging content that resonates with your target audience. This could include blog posts on your website or social media platforms, articles offering helpful tips or industry insights, videos showcasing your products or services in action, tutorials demonstrating how to use your products, or inspiring stories about other young entrepreneurs.

Engaging Your Audience

Building a thriving online presence goes beyond simply creating content. Here's how to engage your audience, build relationships, and foster brand loyalty:

- **Respond to Comments and Messages:** Show your audience you value their input by promptly responding to comments and messages on social media and your website. Address their questions, concerns, and feedback in a courteous and helpful manner.
- **Run Contests and Giveaways:** Create excitement and encourage audience participation by running contests and giveaways that align with your brand. Offer prizes related to your products or services, and ensure the entry requirements promote user-generated content or brand awareness.

- **Collaborate with Micro-Influencers:** Partner with social media influencers with a smaller but highly engaged following that aligns with your target audience. These collaborations can introduce your brand to a new audience and leverage the influencer's credibility to build trust with potential customers.
- **Promote User-Generated Content:** Encourage your audience to share their experiences with your brand by hosting photo contests or featuring customer testimonials on your website and social media platforms. This social proof builds trust and authenticity, and incentivizes others to try your products or services.

- **Host Online Events:** Organize virtual workshops, Q&A sessions, or live chats with industry experts or other young entrepreneurs. This interactive format allows you to connect with your audience on a deeper level, provide valuable information, and establish yourself as a thought leader in your niche.
- **Leverage Email Marketing:** Build an email list by offering valuable content downloads, exclusive discounts, or early access to new products in exchange for email addresses. Use email marketing to nurture leads, share updates about your business, and promote your latest offerings directly to a targeted audience. Maintain a consistent email schedule and prioritize providing value over solely promotional content.
- **Be Authentic and Transparent:** Don't be afraid to show the real you behind the brand. Share your entrepreneurial journey, the challenges you've faced, and the lessons you've learned. This vulnerability fosters trust and connection with your audience, who can relate to your experiences and appreciate your authenticity.

Additional Strategies for You

For the ambitious teen entrepreneur looking to take their online presence to the next level, here are some advanced strategies to consider:

- **Search Engine Optimization (SEO):** Optimize your website and content to rank higher in search engine results pages (SERPs) for relevant keywords. This increases organic traffic and drives potential customers to your website who are actively searching for products or services like yours.
- **Paid Advertising:** Explore paid advertising platforms like Google Ads or Facebook Ads to target your ideal customer with laser precision. Create compelling ad campaigns that showcase your brand message and value proposition, driving targeted traffic to your website or landing pages.
- **Social Media Listening:** Utilize social media listening tools to monitor brand mentions, track industry trends, and understand customer sentiment. This allows you to identify areas for improvement, address customer concerns promptly, and engage in conversations happening around your brand online.
- **Affiliate Marketing:** Partner with other businesses or influencers to promote your products or services in exchange for a commission on each sale generated through their referral link. This expands your reach, leverages the credibility of your partners, and creates a win-win situation for all parties involved.

Crafting a strong brand voice and establishing a compelling online presence is crucial for any teen entrepreneur looking to build a successful business. By understanding your audience, developing a distinct voice that resonates with them, and creating engaging content across the right platforms, you can build a thriving online community and attract customers eager to support your brand.

PART 2

Financial Management and Others

CHAPTER 5

MANAGING YOUR MONEY LIKE A PRO

TRACKING INCOME AND EXPENSES WITH SIMPLE SYSTEMS

Financial literacy is the cornerstone of any successful business, regardless of age. As a teen entrepreneur, keeping track of your income and expenses is not just good practice – it's essential for understanding your financial health, making informed decisions, and ultimately achieving financial self-sufficiency.

Why Track Your Finances?

Beyond the basic task of recording your income and expenses, tracking your finances offers a multitude of benefits for your business:

- **Understanding Your Profitability:** By tracking income and expenses, you can calculate your profit margin – the difference between what you earn and what you spend. Knowing your profitability helps you assess the financial viability of your business and identify areas for improvement. Imagine you sell handmade friendship bracelets for $5 each. You track your materials cost at $1 per bracelet and record $30 in sales over a weekend. This tells you that you made a profit of $2 per bracelet ($5 selling price - $1 material cost) and a total profit of $60 for the weekend ($2 profit/bracelet x 30 bracelets).
- **Making Informed Decisions:** Financial tracking provides valuable data to guide your business decisions. For example, knowing your top-selling product allows you to invest in more inventory, while

identifying high operating costs prompts you to explore cost-saving measures. Let's say your financial tracking reveals that your beaded friendship bracelets consistently sell out, while your braided ones haven't generated much interest. This data suggests focusing your efforts and resources on producing more beaded bracelets to meet customer demand.

- **Tax Preparation Made Easy:** Keeping accurate records of your income and expenses simplifies tax filing come tax season. You'll have all the necessary documentation readily available to ensure accurate tax reporting. Imagine tax season arrives, and you meticulously tracked your income from bracelet sales and any business-related expenses like craft supplies. This organized record-keeping saves you time and ensures you report your business income correctly.
- **Budgeting for Growth:** Financial tracking helps you create a realistic budget for your business. You can allocate funds for marketing, inventory, and potential future investments, ensuring your business has the resources needed for growth. Perhaps you dream of expanding your bracelet business by selling at local craft fairs. Financial tracking allows you to see how much you earn and spend, enabling you to budget for booth fees, marketing materials, and additional supplies to prepare for the fair.

Finding Your Tracking Fit

There's no one-size-fits-all approach to financial tracking. The right system for you depends on your personal preferences, business complexity, and level of comfort with technology. Here are some popular options to consider:

- **The Classic Pen and Paper Method:** A simple notebook or spreadsheet allows you to record your income (sales) and expenses (costs) along with the date and a brief description. For example, you might record "June 1st - Income: Bracelet Sales ($30)" and "June 1st - Expense: Craft Supplies ($10)". This low-tech method is user-friendly and easily accessible, but can be cumbersome for businesses with a high volume of transactions. Imagine managing a thriving online business with hundreds of daily sales – a notebook might become overwhelming.

- **Mobile Apps:** Numerous free and paid mobile apps are designed specifically for expense tracking. These apps offer features like transaction categorization (automatically classifying your expenses as marketing, inventory, etc.), receipt scanning (eliminating the need for paper receipts), and automatic reports (providing insights into your spending habits). Popular options include Mint, YNAB (You Need a Budget), and PocketGuard. These apps are ideal for busy teens who can easily track their finances on the go, snapping a picture of a receipt with their phone instead of manually entering data.
- **Spreadsheet Software:** Programs like Microsoft Excel or Google Sheets offer powerful spreadsheet functionalities for managing your finances. You can create custom templates to record income, expenses, and additional details like product names or customer information. You can also categorize expenses, use formulas to automatically calculate totals and profit margins, and generate detailed reports on your business performance, such as monthly sales trends or top-selling products. While offering more flexibility than mobile apps, spreadsheets require a bit more technical know-how.
- **Accounting Software:** For complex businesses with a high volume of transactions, dedicated accounting software might be a worthwhile investment. These robust platforms offer comprehensive features like inventory management, invoicing (sending bills to

customers), and payroll processing (managing employee salaries). However, accounting software typically comes with a monthly subscription fee. Popular options include QuickBooks and FreshBooks. While not essential for most businesses starting out, these platforms could be beneficial for ventures with a large customer base or complex financial needs.

Implementing Your Tracking System

Once you've chosen your preferred tracking system, it's time to set it up and start recording your business finances. Here's how to get started, regardless of the method you choose:

1. **Create Separate Accounts:** Maintain clear separation between your personal finances and your business finances. Open a dedicated business bank account, even if it's a simple checking account at your local bank. Deposit all your income from your business (sales revenue) into this account and use it to pay all your business expenses (costs associated with running your business). This separation makes tracking your business finances much easier. Imagine you use your personal savings to buy craft supplies and then sell bracelets, depositing the sales cash back into your savings account. This makes it difficult to distinguish between your personal and business finances.
2. **Record Every Transaction:** Develop the habit of recording every single income and expense related to your business, no matter how small. Consistency is key. This includes income from sales, any interest earned on your business bank account, and even refunds you might receive. On the expense side, record everything you spend on your business, from raw materials and supplies to marketing costs and website hosting fees.
3. **Categorize Transactions:** Classify your expenses into meaningful categories. This helps you analyze

where your money is going and identify areas for potential cost savings. Common expense categories include:
    - **Inventory:** Cost of materials used to create your products.
    - **Marketing:** Expenses related to promoting your business, like website fees, social media advertising, or printing flyers.
    - **Supplies:** Any additional supplies needed to run your business, such as packaging materials, shipping boxes, or a printer for invoices.
    - **Transportation:** Costs associated with delivering products to customers or traveling to purchase supplies.
    - **Technology:** Expenses related to software subscriptions, website hosting, or a phone used primarily for business purposes.
    - **Miscellaneous:** Any other expenses that don't fit into the above categories.
4. **Schedule Regular Reviews:** Set aside time each week or month to review your financial records. Analyze your income, expenses, and profitability to gain insights into your business performance. Here are some questions to consider during your review:
    - **What is my total income for this period?**
    - **What are my biggest expenses?**
    - **Are there any areas where I can cut back on costs?**
    - **What are my best-selling products or services?**
    - **Am I on track to meet my financial goals?**

By regularly reviewing your financial data, you can identify trends, make informed decisions, and adjust your business strategy as needed.

Advanced Tracking Tips

As your business grows and your financial transactions become more complex, consider implementing these advanced tracking tips:

- **Utilize Receipt Scanning Apps:** Mobile apps allow you to scan receipts directly into your tracking software, eliminating the need for physical record-keeping. This saves time, reduces the risk of losing receipts, and ensures your expense data is accurate and readily accessible.
- **Set Up Automatic Transactions:** Schedule recurring expenses like website hosting fees or subscription services to be automatically deducted from your business bank account. This ensures timely payments and avoids late fees. Imagine forgetting to renew your website domain name – automatic payments prevent service interruptions and potential website downtime.
- **Track Inventory Levels:** Maintain a system for tracking your inventory – the products you have on hand to sell. This helps you avoid stockouts (running out of popular products) and optimize your ordering process. You can use a simple spreadsheet or inventory management software to track your inventory levels, ensuring you have enough supplies to meet customer demand without overstocking and wasting money.
- **Separate Business and Personal Expenses:** Be diligent about keeping your business and personal expenses separate. This is crucial for accurate financial reporting and tax purposes. Avoid using your business bank account for personal purchases or vice versa. This keeps your records clean and simplifies tax filing come April.

Building a Financial Tracking Habit

Developing a consistent financial tracking habit is essential for the success of your business. Here are some tips to make it easier:

- **Start Small:** Don't overwhelm yourself with a complex system right away. Begin with a simple notebook or a user-friendly mobile app.
- **Set Reminders:** Schedule recurring reminders on your phone or calendar to record your income and expenses daily or weekly.
- **Make it a Routine:** Integrate financial tracking into your daily or weekly business routine. This could be the first thing you do each morning or the last thing before bed.

- **Celebrate Milestones:** Acknowledge and reward yourself for staying consistent with your financial tracking. This could be a small treat or simply recognizing your progress. Positive reinforcement helps maintain motivation and keeps you on track.
- **Embrace Technology:** Leverage technology to simplify financial tracking. Utilize mobile apps for on-the-go recording, explore online tutorials for spreadsheet software, or consider cloud-based accounting software for data security and accessibility.
- **Seek Help When Needed:** Don't be afraid to seek help from a parent, guardian, or trusted adult familiar with basic bookkeeping practices. They can guide you in setting up your tracking system or answer any questions you might have.

By establishing a system for tracking your income and expenses, you gain invaluable insights into the financial health of your business. This empowers you to make informed decisions, optimize your resource allocation, and ultimately achieve your entrepreneurial goals. Remember that financial literacy is a journey, not a destination. As your business evolves, so too will your financial tracking needs. Embrace the learning process, adapt your systems as needed, and watch your business flourish with the power of financial knowledge.

BUDGETING FOR GROWTH AND REINVESTMENT

Congratulations. You've launched your business, mastered the art of financial tracking (as detailed in the previous section), and are generating income. But a successful business doesn't stop there. To achieve true financial self-sufficiency and propel your venture towards long-term growth, you need a strategic plan for budgeting and reinvesting your profits.

Understanding Budgeting

A budget is a financial blueprint that outlines your income and expenses for a specific period, typically a month, quarter, or year. For your business, it's a roadmap guiding your financial decisions and resource allocation. Here's why budgeting is crucial for growth and reinvestment:

- **Prioritizing Expenses:** A budget helps you identify and prioritize your business expenses. It ensures you allocate funds towards essential operational costs like supplies or marketing, while leaving room for reinvestment opportunities. Imagine you run a dog walking service. Your budget might prioritize dog waste bags, leashes, and insurance, while still allocating funds for flyers or online advertising to attract new clients.
- **Making Informed Decisions:** By understanding your income and expenses, you can make informed decisions about your business. For example, let's say

your budget reveals that your dog walking service has high profitability, but your homemade dog treat business is struggling. Based on this data, you can decide to invest more resources in marketing your dog walking service or consider revamping your dog treat recipe to improve sales.

- **Setting Financial Goals:** The budgeting process helps you define clear financial goals for your business. Do you want to increase your dog walking clientele by 20% in the next quarter? Expand your dog treat offerings to include new flavors within the next year? A budget helps you track your progress towards achieving these goals. Perhaps your goal is to save a specific amount of profit each month to reinvest in a professional website for your dog walking service.
- **Facilitating Reinvestment:** The ultimate purpose of budgeting is to create a sustainable financial foundation that allows you to reinvest profits back into your business. This reinvestment fuels growth, propelling your venture towards future success. By strategically allocating funds in your budget for reinvestment, you ensure your business has the resources needed to flourish.

Crafting Your Budget

Now that you understand the importance of budgeting, let's delve into the process of creating a budget for your business:

1. **Gather Your Financial Data:** The first step is to gather your financial data. This includes your income from sales (dog walking fees and dog treat sales in our example), any interest earned on your business bank account, and a detailed record of all your business expenses categorized as per the methods outlined in the previous chapter (inventory, marketing, supplies, transportation, etc.). Having all your financial

information readily available allows you to create a realistic and accurate budget.

2. **Estimate Future Income:** Based on your current sales trends and any anticipated changes (like seasonal fluctuations or marketing campaigns you plan to launch), estimate your projected income for the budgeting period. Be realistic but optimistic – don't underestimate your potential for growth. Perhaps you anticipate an increase in dog walking clients during the summer months due to busier schedules for pet owners. Factor this potential increase into your projected income for the upcoming quarter.
3. **Identify Fixed and Variable Expenses:** Distinguish between fixed expenses (costs that remain constant each period, like monthly website hosting fees for your dog walking service) and variable expenses (costs that fluctuate based on your business activity, like the cost of dog waste bags or dog treat ingredients). Understanding this distinction allows you to allocate funds more efficiently. For example, you can set aside a fixed amount each month for website hosting, while allocating a variable amount for dog waste bags based on the number of clients you serve.
4. **Allocate Funds for Operational Costs:** Allocate funds in your budget to cover all essential operational costs associated with running your business. This includes fixed expenses like website hosting or rent for a physical storefront (if applicable), variable expenses like supplies or advertising, and any other costs necessary for day-to-day operations like transportation to dog walking appointments or phone service for client communication.
5. **Set Aside Funds for Reinvestment:** The key to growth lies in reinvestment. After allocating funds for operational costs, dedicate a portion of your budget to reinvestment. This could involve investing in new inventory (purchasing additional dog leashes or treat

ingredients), expanding your marketing efforts (creating eye-catching flyers or running targeted online ads), upgrading your equipment (purchasing a professional dog grooming kit), or acquiring new skills through educational resources (taking an online course on dog training to enhance your dog walking service offerings). The specific reinvestment strategies you choose will depend on your business goals and current needs.

Reinvestment Strategies

Here are some specific strategies for reinvesting your profits and propelling your business towards growth, using our dog walking service example:

- **Inventory Expansion:** Reinvest in expanding your inventory to cater to a wider range of clients. This could involve purchasing different sized leashes and harnesses to accommodate various dog breeds, acquiring specialized equipment for handling senior dogs or dogs with behavioral challenges, or stocking a variety of dog treat flavors to cater to different preferences.
- **Marketing and Advertising:** Allocate budget towards marketing and advertising initiatives to reach a wider audience and attract new customers. Explore options like creating eye-catching flyers or business cards to distribute at local pet stores or veterinary clinics. Consider social media marketing, running targeted online ads in your local area, or developing a referral program to incentivize existing clients to recommend your dog walking service to their network.
- **Business Technology:** Invest in technology that can streamline your business operations and improve efficiency. Consider scheduling software to manage your dog walking appointments, GPS tracking devices

for added pet safety and client peace of mind, or a customer relationship management (CRM) system to store client information and preferences.

- **Personal and Professional Development:** As the CEO of your business, your knowledge and skills are essential for its success. Reinvest in yourself by attending workshops or conferences related to pet care or business management. Take online courses on dog training or pet first aid to enhance your service offerings. Purchase books or resources on entrepreneurship or customer service to refine your business acumen. The knowledge and skills you gain can be directly applied to improve the quality of your dog walking service and attract more clients.
- **Contingency Planning:** Allocate a portion of your budget for unexpected expenses or potential setbacks. This could include emergency veterinary care for a client's dog while in your care, liability insurance to protect your business, or funds set aside to cover repairs or replacements for equipment like leashes or dog waste bag dispensers. Having a financial buffer ensures your business can weather unforeseen circumstances and maintain stability.

Striking the Right Reinvestment Ratio

There's no one-size-fits-all answer to how much you should reinvest. The ideal reinvestment ratio depends on your business stage, goals, and risk tolerance.

- **Early Stage Businesses:** If you're a new business owner, focus on reinvesting a higher percentage of your profits back into the business. This could be 70% or more allocated towards operational costs and reinvestment strategies like marketing and inventory expansion to establish a strong foundation for growth.

- **Established Businesses:** As your business matures and generates consistent income, you can adjust your reinvestment ratio. Perhaps you allocate 50% towards operational costs and reinvestment, and the remaining 50% towards profit that can be used for personal savings or future business ventures.
- **Risk Tolerance:** Consider your risk tolerance when determining your reinvestment ratio. If you're comfortable with taking calculated risks, you might allocate a larger portion of your profits towards reinvestment strategies with the potential for high returns, like expanding into new service offerings or launching a targeted marketing campaign. If you prefer a more cautious approach, prioritize reinvesting in areas that ensure stability and minimize risk, like building a loyal customer base or maintaining a healthy cash reserve.

Keeping Your Budget on Track

Creating a budget is just the first step. It's crucial to monitor your progress and adapt your budget as needed throughout the budgeting period. Here's how:

- **Track Your Actual Expenses:** Keep meticulous records of your actual expenses throughout the budgeting period. Compare your actual spending to your budgeted amounts for each category.
- **Analyze Variances:** Identify any significant discrepancies between your budgeted and actual expenses. For example, if your dog waste bag expenses are consistently exceeding your budget allocation, explore ways to reduce costs, like purchasing in bulk or finding a more economical supplier.
- **Adjust Your Budget:** Based on your analysis, make adjustments to your budget as necessary. This might

involve reallocating funds between different categories or revising your overall income or expense projections.

- **Review and Revise Regularly:** Schedule regular reviews of your budget, perhaps monthly or quarterly. This allows you to adapt to changing circumstances, ensure your budget remains realistic, and continue making informed financial decisions for your thriving business.

By following these steps and embracing a growth mindset, you can utilize budgeting and reinvestment as powerful tools to propel your business towards long-term success. Remember that financial literacy is a journey, not a destination. As your business evolves, so too will your budgeting needs. Embrace the learning process, adapt your strategies as needed, and watch your business flourish with the power of financial knowledge.

Advanced Budgeting and Reinvestment Strategies for Savvy Teen Entrepreneurs

As your business matures and you gain experience, consider incorporating these advanced budgeting and reinvestment strategies:

- **Cash Flow Forecasting:** Move beyond static budgets and delve into cash flow forecasting. This involves predicting future cash inflows (income) and outflows (expenses) to gain a more dynamic understanding of your business's financial health. Cash flow forecasting helps you anticipate potential shortfalls and make informed decisions about resource allocation. Imagine you project a temporary dip in income due to a seasonal slowdown in dog walking services. Cash flow forecasting allows you to plan ahead and adjust your budget accordingly, perhaps by reducing non-essential expenses or utilizing your contingency fund to maintain financial stability.

- **Scenario Planning:** Develop different budget scenarios to prepare for various possibilities. Create a "best-case scenario" budget outlining your financial projections if your dog walking service experiences a surge in new clients. Contrast this with a "worst-case scenario" budget anticipating a decline in business activity. Having these scenarios mapped out allows you to be proactive and make adjustments to your budget or reinvestment strategies as needed, regardless of the circumstances.
- **Profit Margin Analysis:** Track your profit margin – the difference between your selling price and your cost of goods sold – over time. This helps you identify areas for improvement and optimize your pricing strategies. By analyzing your profit margin for dog walking services and dog treat sales, you can determine if a price increase is necessary to maintain profitability or if exploring alternative suppliers for dog walking equipment or treat ingredients can help reduce costs and improve your profit margin.
- **Long-Term Reinvestment Planning:** Look beyond immediate reinvestment needs and start planning for the long-term future of your business. Perhaps you dream of expanding your dog walking service into a full-fledged pet care business offering additional services like pet sitting or dog training. Allocate a portion of your budget towards long-term reinvestment goals, such as saving for additional training or certifications, or researching potential business partnerships to support your expansion plans.

By mastering the art of budgeting and reinvestment, you plant the seeds for long-term success in your business. Remember that a well-crafted budget serves as a roadmap, guiding your financial decisions and ensuring your business has the resources needed to flourish. Strategic reinvestment fuels growth, propelling your venture towards achieving your entrepreneurial goals.

UNDERSTANDING BASIC TAX RESPONSIBILITIES

With the thrill of turning a profit often comes the question: what about taxes? Understanding your basic tax responsibilities is crucial for any business owner, regardless of age. In this section, we will discuss the knowledge and resources you will need to navigate the tax landscape for your business, ensuring you comply with regulations and avoid any unwanted surprises come tax season.

Why Do Teens Need to Pay Taxes?

The short answer is – it depends. In many countries, teenagers are considered dependents of their parents or guardians for tax purposes. However, if your business generates income that exceeds a certain threshold, you may be required to file a separate tax return and pay taxes on your earnings. Here's a breakdown of the key factors that determine your tax filing obligations:

- **Income Threshold:** Each country establishes a minimum income threshold for filing a tax return. This threshold can vary significantly. For example, in the United States, a single filer under the age of 19 typically doesn't need to file a tax return if their gross income (total income before expenses) is below $12,550 (as of 2024). However, it's always a good practice to check the latest tax regulations in your area, even if your income falls below the threshold. Some countries might have lower thresholds or different rules for income earned by minors operating businesses.

- **Business Structure:** The legal structure of your business can also impact your tax obligations. For example, sole proprietorships (businesses owned and operated by a single person) typically report business income on their personal tax return. In contrast, other business structures like partnerships or corporations might require separate tax filings for the business entity itself. The legal and tax implications of different business structures can vary by location. If you're considering establishing a business structure beyond a sole proprietorship, consult with a legal or tax professional familiar with regulations for businesses owned by minors in your area.

Understanding Taxable Income:

Not all the income your business generates is necessarily taxable. Here's what you need to know about taxable income for your business:

- **Gross Income:** This refers to the total revenue your business generates from sales or services rendered.
- **Business Expenses:** You can deduct legitimate business expenses from your gross income to arrive at your taxable income. These expenses could include a wide range of costs directly related to running your business. Here are some specific examples:
    - **Supplies:** Materials used to create your products (fabric for clothing, ingredients for baked goods, art supplies for a crafts business)
    - **Marketing:** Costs associated with promoting your business (advertising on social media platforms, printing flyers, creating a website)
    - **Equipment Rental:** Rental fees for equipment necessary for your business operations (camera equipment for photography services, a rental booth at a craft fair)

- **Website Hosting Fees:** Costs associated with maintaining a website for your business (domain name registration, website hosting plan fees)
- **Bank Charges:** Fees associated with your business bank account (monthly maintenance fees, transaction fees)

It's important to note that not all expenses are created equal. Some countries might have limitations on certain deductions, particularly for business owners who operate their businesses out of their homes. For example, deductions for home office expenses might be restricted. Always consult the tax regulations in your area or seek guidance from a tax professional to ensure you're claiming deductions accurately.

- **Taxable Income:** Your taxable income is essentially your gross income minus all your deductible business expenses. This is the figure you'll use to calculate any taxes owed on your business earnings.

Tax Forms and Filing Deadlines:

The specific tax forms and deadlines will vary depending on your location. Here's a general overview of what you might expect:

- **Tax Forms:** The government agency responsible for tax collection will typically provide specific tax forms for filing your business income. These forms might be separate from your personal tax return forms, depending on your business structure. For example, in the United States, a sole proprietor operating a business might file a Schedule C form attached to their personal tax return (Form 1040) to report their business income and expenses.

- **Filing Deadlines:** Tax filing deadlines also vary by location. Ensure you file your tax return and pay any taxes owed before the designated deadline to avoid penalties or interest charges. Missing tax deadlines can result in significant financial repercussions. In the United States, the deadline to file federal income taxes is typically April 15th of the following year, although extensions might be available under certain circumstances.

Seeking Help When Needed:

Navigating the tax system can seem daunting, especially for a first-time business owner. Here are some resources to help you comply with your tax obligations:

- **Government Websites:** Most government tax agencies have dedicated sections on their websites offering resources for small businesses or self-employed individuals. These resources often include tax guides, downloadable forms, and frequently asked questions (FAQs) to help you understand your tax responsibilities. For example, in the United States, the Internal Revenue Service (IRS) website offers a wealth of information specifically tailored to small businesses, including a section dedicated to self-employed individuals: https://www.irs.gov/businesses/small-businesses-self-employed/self-employed-individuals-tax-center
- **Tax Professionals:** Consider consulting with a qualified tax professional familiar with tax regulations for businesses owned by minors. They can provide personalized guidance specific to your situation and income level. A tax professional can help you:
    - Determine your exact tax filing obligations based on your business structure and income.

- Identify all eligible business deductions to minimize your taxable income.
- Choose the appropriate tax forms and ensure your return is filed accurately and on time.
- Navigate any complexities associated with taxes, such as estimated tax payments (discussed later).

Finding a tax professional doesn't have to break the bank. Many accountants or tax preparers offer consultations or discounted rates for students or young entrepreneurs. Consider asking family or friends for recommendations or searching online for qualified professionals in your area.

RECORD KEEPING

Maintaining accurate and meticulous records of your business income and expenses is crucial for tax filing. These records not only ensure you claim all your eligible deductions, but also serve as proof of your income in case of an audit. Here are some best practices for record keeping:

- **Separate Accounts:** Open a dedicated business bank account to track all your business income and expenses. This separation from your personal finances simplifies record keeping and makes tax preparation easier. Having a dedicated business account also strengthens the legitimacy of your business in the eyes of tax authorities.
- **Receipt Collection:** Develop the habit of collecting receipts for all your business-related purchases. These receipts serve as proof of your expenses and are essential for claiming deductions on your tax return. Consider using a designated folder or digital filing system to organize your receipts throughout the year.
- **Track Your Income:** Maintain a system for recording all your business income, whether it's cash

sales, online transactions, or payments received from clients. This could involve a simple notebook, a spreadsheet, or dedicated accounting software. Tracking your income consistently ensures you have a complete picture of your earnings come tax season.

- **Digital Tools:** Explore digital tools like accounting software or spreadsheet templates designed to track business income and expenses. These tools can streamline your record keeping and save you time and effort come tax season. Many user-friendly accounting software programs offer free trials or affordable plans for small businesses.

Advanced Tax Considerations for Growing Businesses

As your business matures and generates significant income, you might encounter more complex tax considerations. Here are some additional points to keep in mind:

- **Estimated Taxes:** In some countries, businesses with high projected tax bills might be required to pay estimated taxes throughout the year. These estimated payments ensure a steady flow of tax revenue to the government and prevent a large tax bill at the end of the year. For example, in the United States, self-employed individuals with a projected tax liability of $1,000 or more are generally required to make estimated tax payments quarterly. Consult the tax regulations in your area to determine if estimated tax payments apply to your business.
- **Self-Employment Taxes:** Beyond income taxes, some countries might also require self-employed individuals (including business owners) to pay additional taxes to cover social security or Medicare contributions. These taxes are typically calculated as a percentage of your net income (taxable income) after

deductions. Understanding your self-employment tax obligations is crucial for accurate tax filing and avoiding any unexpected charges.

- **State and Local Taxes:** In addition to federal taxes, some states or localities within a country might also impose their own taxes on business income. Research the tax regulations in your specific location to determine if any state or local taxes apply to your business.

Remember: Tax laws and regulations can be complex and change frequently. This chapter provides a general overview of tax considerations for businesses. Always consult the latest tax regulations in your area and seek guidance from a qualified tax professional when needed. By staying informed and taking the necessary steps to comply with tax requirements, you can ensure your business operates smoothly and avoids any potential tax-related issues.

While navigating the tax system might seem daunting at first, understanding the basics equips you to develop proactive strategies for managing your business's tax obligations. Here are some tips to consider:

- **Track Your Finances Year-Round:** Don't wait until tax season to scramble and gather records. Develop a system for tracking your business income and expenses throughout the year. This consistent approach ensures you have all the necessary information readily available come filing time.
- **Maximize Deductions:** Stay informed about eligible business deductions in your area. Explore resources from government tax websites or consult with a tax professional to identify all potential deductions that can reduce your taxable income. Remember that the more deductions you can claim, the lower your overall tax liability will be.

- **Save for Taxes:** Taxes are an inevitable business expense. Set aside a portion of your business income each month or quarter specifically for tax payments. This proactive approach ensures you have the funds readily available when tax deadlines approach and avoids scrambling at the last minute.
- **Consider Tax Implications of Business Decisions:** As your business grows, consider the tax implications of your decisions. For example, if you're contemplating hiring employees, research payroll taxes and other associated costs. Planning ahead and factoring in potential tax liabilities allows you to make informed choices that optimize your business's financial health.
- **Stay Organized:** Develop a system for organizing your business receipts, invoices, and other financial documents. This organization will save you time and frustration during tax season. Consider using digital filing systems or cloud storage solutions to keep your records accessible and secure.
- **File Electronically:** Many tax agencies offer electronic filing options for tax returns. Filing electronically streamlines the process, reduces the risk of errors, and allows you to receive faster refunds (if applicable).

The Benefits of Responsible Tax Management:

By taking a proactive approach to tax compliance, you reap a multitude of benefits for your business:

- **Peace of Mind:** Knowing you've fulfilled your tax obligations fosters peace of mind and allows you to focus on growing your business without the worry of potential penalties or audits.
- **Builds Trust and Credibility:** Responsible tax management demonstrates your commitment to

operating a legitimate business. This can enhance your credibility in the eyes of clients, partners, and potential investors.

- **Avoids Penalties and Interest Charges:** Missing tax deadlines or filing inaccurate returns can result in significant penalties and interest charges. Proactive tax management ensures you avoid these financial burdens.
- **Establishes a Strong Financial Foundation:** Developing good tax habits early on lays a solid foundation for responsible financial management as your business continues to grow and evolve.

Understanding and managing your tax responsibilities is an essential part of running a successful business. This chapter has equipped you with the knowledge and resources to navigate the tax landscape with confidence. Remember that staying informed, seeking guidance when needed, and adopting proactive strategies will ensure your business thrives while remaining compliant with all tax regulations. As your business flourishes, celebrate your achievements while keeping a responsible eye on your tax obligations. With dedication and a strategic approach, you can ensure your business soars to new heights of financial success.

CHAPTER 6

SAVING, INVESTING, AND BUILDING WEALTH

SETTING FINANCIAL GOALS FOR THE FUTURE

The thrill of turning a profit is invigorating, but true financial success goes beyond immediate earnings. Setting clear, achievable financial goals for the future is crucial for ensuring your business thrives in the long run.

Why Set Financial Goals?

Financial goals serve as a roadmap for your business's financial future. They provide direction, focus your efforts, and motivate you to make smart financial decisions. Here's how setting financial goals benefits your teen business:

- **Clarity and Direction:** Financial goals help you define what success looks like for your business. Do you dream of expanding your product line, hiring additional employees, or opening a physical storefront? Clearly defined goals provide a target and keep you moving in the right direction. Imagine you run a dog walking service. Your long-term goal might be to expand into a full-fledged pet care business offering pet sitting and dog training. Setting financial goals for acquiring the necessary equipment, certifications, and potential marketing strategies provides a roadmap for achieving this vision.
- **Improved Decision-Making:** With specific goals in mind, you'll be better equipped to make informed financial decisions. Every investment, expense, or pricing strategy can be evaluated through the lens of whether it aligns with your long-term financial

aspirations. For example, if your goal is to increase your profit margin for your dog walking service, you might consider raising your rates slightly or exploring cost-saving measures like negotiating bulk discounts with pet supply stores for waste removal bags or treats.

- **Increased Motivation:** Financial goals provide a sense of purpose and fuel your motivation. Knowing you're working towards achieving something tangible can keep you energized and committed, especially during challenging times. Setting a goal to save a specific amount for a new marketing campaign for your dog walking service can give you the motivation to hustle and secure new clients, knowing the increased revenue will contribute directly to achieving your goal.
- **Enhanced Financial Discipline:** Setting goals encourages you to develop habits that promote financial health. This might involve budgeting more effectively, saving a portion of your profits for future investments, or exploring cost-saving measures within your business operations. For instance, a goal to establish an emergency fund for your dog walking service might prompt you to adopt stricter budgeting practices to ensure a portion of your earnings are consistently set aside for unexpected expenses like equipment repair or cancellations due to inclement weather.

Types of Financial Goals for Your Business

Financial goals for your business can encompass various aspects of its financial health. Here are some key categories to consider, along with specific examples for a business owner:

- **Growth and Expansion:** Do you envision scaling your business by offering new products or services? Setting goals for market expansion, hiring employees, or increasing sales volume can propel your business to the next level. For your dog walking service, a growth goal could be expanding your service area to include a neighboring community, requiring additional marketing efforts and potentially hiring another dog walker.

- **Profitability:** Every business thrives on healthy profits. Setting goals for increasing your profit margin, reducing operational costs, or diversifying your income streams ensures your business remains financially sustainable in the long run. A profitability goal for your dog walking service might be to increase your profit margin by 10% within the next six months. To achieve this, you could explore offering premium services like extended walks or group walks at a slightly higher rate, or consider partnering with a local pet store to offer bundled services.
- **Financial Security:** Building a financial safety net is crucial for any business. Setting goals for establishing an emergency fund or saving for future equipment purchases can safeguard your business against unexpected challenges. For your dog walking service, a financial security goal could be to accumulate a specific amount in an emergency fund to cover unexpected expenses like vet bills for your own pet or repairs to your walking equipment.
- **Financial Independence:** As a teen entrepreneur, your business can be a vehicle towards achieving financial independence. Setting goals for generating income that allows you to cover your personal expenses or contribute to your education fosters a sense of self-reliance and empowers you to take control of your financial future. A financial independence goal for your dog walking service might be to generate enough income to cover your monthly phone bill or contribute a specific amount towards your college savings fund.

Crafting SMART Goals for Sustainable Success

Not all goals are created equal. Effective financial goals for your business should be SMART:

- **Specific:** Vague goals lack direction. Instead of aiming to "make more money," define a specific target – "increase sales from dog walking services by 20% in the next quarter."

- **Measurable:** Track your progress towards your goals. Set quantifiable benchmarks – "save $100 per week for a new marketing campaign for my dog walking service."
- **Attainable:** Aim high, but ensure your goals are realistic and achievable within a defined timeframe. Consider your current resources and market conditions when setting your targets. For instance, if you're a new dog walker with a limited client base, aiming to increase sales by 500% in a month might be unrealistic. A more attainable goal might be to secure 5 new clients within the next 3 months.
- **Relevant:** Align your financial goals with your overall business vision. Don't set goals solely for the sake of having them. Ensure they contribute to the long-term success of your dog walking service. For example, a goal to win "Best Pet Service Provider" in a local community award program might not be directly relevant to your financial goals. However, a goal to increase customer satisfaction through offering referral bonuses for new clients could be relevant as it can lead to increased sales and a more sustainable business.
- **Time-Bound:** Establish deadlines for achieving your goals. This creates a sense of urgency and keeps you accountable. Set short-term milestones within your long-term goals to maintain momentum. For your dog walking service, a time-bound goal could be to "save $400 for a new marketing campaign within the next 3

months." This goal can be further broken down into weekly or monthly savings targets to ensure you stay on track.

Developing Your Financial Roadmap:

Now that you understand the types of financial goals and the importance of setting SMART goals, it's time to create your roadmap for financial success with your teen business. Here's a step-by-step process you can follow for your dog walking service or any other teen venture:

1. **Brainstorm and Reflect:** Take time to brainstorm your financial aspirations for your business. Where do you see it in the next year, five years, or even ten years? Consider your long-term vision and jot down all your financial dreams, no matter how ambitious they might seem at first glance. Do you dream of offering pet boarding services alongside dog walking? Do you envision expanding your service area to cover the entire city? Write down everything!
2. **Prioritize and Refine:** Once you have a comprehensive list of goals, prioritize them based on their importance and urgency. Focus on achieving one or two high-impact goals at a time. For your dog walking service, a high-impact goal might be to increase your client base, as this directly translates to increased revenue. Refine your goals using the SMART criteria to ensure they are clear, measurable, achievable, relevant, and time-bound.
3. **Break Down Large Goals:** Large, long-term goals can feel overwhelming. Break them down into smaller, more manageable milestones. For example, if your long-term goal is to offer pet boarding services, a smaller milestone could be to research local regulations and licensing requirements for pet boarding businesses. Another milestone could be to

save a specific amount of money for initial startup costs associated with pet boarding, like additional pet insurance or modifying your living space to accommodate overnight guests.

4. **Develop Action Plans:** For each of your SMART goals, create a specific action plan outlining the steps you need to take to achieve them. This action plan for your dog walking service might involve identifying marketing strategies to reach new clients, such as creating flyers or social media campaigns targeted towards pet owners in your neighborhood. It could also involve researching and implementing a system for online appointment booking and secure payment processing to streamline your operations and attract tech-savvy clients.
5. **Track Your Progress and Celebrate Milestones:** Monitor your progress towards your goals regularly. This allows you to identify areas where you're excelling and areas that might need adjustments. Celebrating milestones, big or small, keeps you motivated and reinforces positive financial behaviors. Reaching your goal of saving $400 for a marketing campaign is a cause for celebration! Reward yourself for your dedication and use this milestone as a springboard to propel you towards achieving your next goal.

Building Sustainable Financial Habits:

Setting goals is just the first step. Developing sustainable financial habits is crucial for turning your aspirations into reality for your teen business. Here are some key habits to cultivate:

- **Regular Bookkeeping:** Maintain accurate financial records for your business. This includes tracking your income, expenses, and profits. Regular bookkeeping allows you to monitor your financial health and make informed decisions about your business.

- **Budgeting:** Create a budget that allocates your business income towards expenses and savings goals. Sticking to your budget ensures you don't overspend and ensures you have sufficient funds allocated for growth and unexpected costs. For your dog walking service, a budget might include allocating a portion of your income towards equipment maintenance (leashes, waste bags, treats), marketing expenses (flyers, online advertising), and saving for future investments (additional insurance, pet first-aid training).

- **Frugal Mindset:** Embrace a frugal mindset without sacrificing quality. Look for ways to save on operational costs without compromising the services you offer. This might involve negotiating bulk discounts with pet supply stores for walking essentials, exploring free or low-cost marketing avenues like social media marketing, or bartering services with other local businesses (e.g., offering pet walking discounts to clients who use a specific grooming salon).
- **Continuous Learning:** The business landscape is constantly evolving. Stay curious and commit to continuous learning. Research industry trends, attend workshops or webinars relevant to your business, and connect with other teen entrepreneurs to exchange ideas and best practices. For your dog walking service, this could involve learning about pet CPR and first-aid to enhance your service offerings, researching new pet care trends like positive reinforcement training methods to attract clients, or attending workshops on social media marketing to optimize your online presence.
- **Seeking Mentorship:** Don't be afraid to seek guidance from experienced entrepreneurs or financial

professionals. A mentor can provide valuable insights, offer support, and help you navigate challenges. Consider connecting with local business owners or approaching teachers or school counselors for mentorship opportunities. Financial professionals can offer guidance on tax implications for your teen business, budgeting strategies, and potential investment opportunities.

Remember that financial empowerment is a journey, not a destination. Celebrate your achievements, learn from setbacks, and continuously adapt your strategies to ensure your business thrives and propels you towards a financially secure future.

EXPLORING INVESTMENT OPTIONS FOR TEENS

Now that you're generating profits, you might be considering the exciting world of investing. Investing allows you to put your hard-earned money to work, potentially earning a return that grows your wealth over time.

Understanding the Basics of Investing

Before diving into specific investment options, it's crucial to grasp the fundamental principles of investing. Here are some key concepts to keep in mind:

- **Risk and Return:** There's a fundamental relationship between risk and return. Generally, investments with the potential for higher returns come with a greater degree of risk. Conversely, low-risk investments typically offer lower returns. As a young investor with a longer time horizon (the amount of time you have until you need the money), you might have a higher tolerance for risk, allowing you to explore a wider range of investment options. However, it's important to strike a balance that aligns with your comfort level and specific goals.

- **Time Horizon:** Your time horizon refers to the timeframe you have in mind for your investment goals. Are you saving for a short-term goal like a new computer in a year or a long-term goal like college tuition five years down the line? Knowing your time horizon significantly impacts the types of investments you choose. Generally, long-term goals (5+ years) allow for greater risk tolerance, as the market has more time to recover from fluctuations. Short-term goals (within 5 years) benefit from safer investment options with lower volatility (meaning less fluctuation in price).
- **Diversification:** Don't put all your eggs in one basket! Diversification is a cornerstone of successful investing. Spreading your investments across different asset classes (categories of investments) helps mitigate risk. If one asset class performs poorly, the gains from others might help offset the losses. Here's a breakdown of some common asset classes:
    - **Stocks:** Ownership shares in publicly traded companies. Stocks offer the potential for high returns through capital appreciation (increase in share price) and dividend payments (a portion of a company's profits distributed to shareholders). However, they also carry a higher degree of risk due to market fluctuations.
    - **Bonds:** IOUs issued by governments or corporations. Bondholders essentially loan money to the issuer in exchange for a fixed interest rate paid out over time. Bonds are generally considered less risky than stocks, but they also offer lower potential returns.
    - **Real Estate:** Owning or investing in property can generate income through rent or potential appreciation in value over time. Real estate investment can be complex and requires

significant capital, but it can also offer diversification benefits and a hedge against inflation (the decrease in purchasing power of money over time).
    - **Cash Equivalents:** These are highly liquid (easily convertible to cash) investments with minimal risk. Examples include savings accounts and money market accounts. They offer low returns but provide easy access to your money for short-term needs.

Investment Options for Teenagers

Now that you understand the core principles, let's explore various investment options suitable for young entrepreneurs, categorized based on risk tolerance:

Low-Risk Options:

- **Savings Accounts:** This is a foundational and low-risk option. Savings accounts offer a guaranteed return on your money (interest) and provide easy access to your funds when needed. They are ideal for short-term goals or establishing an emergency fund for your business. Consider high-yield savings accounts that offer a slightly higher interest rate compared to traditional savings accounts. However, keep in mind that interest rates on savings accounts are typically lower than inflation, meaning your purchasing power might decrease slightly over time.
- **Certificates of Deposit (CDs):** CDs offer a fixed interest rate for a predetermined period (typically ranging from a few months to several years). They are generally considered a low-risk option, but your money is locked in for the CD term. This can be beneficial for a long-term goal if you can commit to not needing the money before the CD matures. Early withdrawal often

comes with penalties that eat into your potential earnings. Shop around for CDs with competitive interest rates.

Moderate-Risk Options:

- **Roth IRAs (Individual Retirement Accounts):** While eligibility for traditional IRAs might be limited for teenagers with earned income below a certain threshold, Roth IRAs offer a unique opportunity for young investors with a long-term outlook. Contributions to a Roth IRA are typically made with after-tax dollars, but qualified withdrawals in retirement are tax-free! This can be a fantastic way to jumpstart your long-term retirement savings and benefit from tax-free growth over decades. Keep in mind that there are contribution limits for Roth IRAs, and you might not be eligible to contribute the full amount if your business income falls below a certain threshold.

- **Fractional Shares:** The rise of fractional share investing platforms has opened exciting doors for young investors. These platforms allow you to purchase a fraction of a share in a publicly traded company, making it possible to invest in high-priced stocks that might have been out of reach otherwise. Fractional shares offer diversification and the potential for growth, but Remember that the stock market is inherently risky. Stock prices can fluctuate significantly, and you could potentially lose money on your investment. Do your research on companies before investing in their fractional shares.

Higher-Risk Options:

- **Peer-to-Peer (P2P) Lending:** P2P lending platforms connect borrowers with lenders. As a young investor, you can potentially earn a return by lending money to individuals or businesses. These loans typically carry higher interest rates than traditional savings accounts, but they also come with a higher degree of risk. Borrowers on P2P platforms may have poor creditworthiness, increasing the chance of default (failure to repay the loan). Thoroughly research borrowers and understand the platform's risk mitigation strategies (like loan diversification tools) before investing. Only invest what you can afford to lose, and consider starting with smaller amounts to test the waters.
- **Micro-Investing Apps:** These user-friendly apps allow you to invest small amounts of money regularly, often with automated features for automatic deposits from your checking account. They are a fantastic way to ease into the world of investing and build a long-term investment habit. However, micro-investing apps typically focus on fractional shares or ETFs (Exchange-Traded Funds), which can be volatile in the short term. ETFs are essentially baskets of securities (stocks, bonds, etc.) that track a specific index or sector. They offer diversification and lower fees compared to actively managed mutual funds, but their value can fluctuate based on the underlying assets. Consider your risk tolerance and time horizon before investing through micro-investing apps.

Important Considerations for Young Investors

Before you start investing, here are some crucial points to remember:

- **Parental Guidance (if applicable):** Depending on your age and local regulations, parental involvement or consent might be required for opening investment accounts. Communicate openly with your parents or guardians about your investment goals and explore options together. They might be able to offer valuable insights and guidance based on their own experiences.

- **Financial Literacy:** Investing involves a degree of risk. Educate yourself before putting your money to work. Read books, articles, and online resources about different investment options and strategies. Consider taking online courses or workshops geared towards young investors. The more you know, the better equipped you'll be to make informed decisions.
- **Start Small and Scale Up:** Don't feel pressured to invest a large sum of money right away. Start with a small amount you can comfortably afford and gradually increase your investments as your knowledge and confidence grow. This allows you to test the waters, learn from experience, and minimize potential losses.
- **Seek Professional Advice (Consider Cost vs. Benefit):** While a financial advisor can provide personalized investment guidance, their services often come with a fee. For young investors with limited capital, the cost of financial advice might outweigh the benefits. However, if you're considering more complex investment strategies or have a significant amount of money to invest, consulting with a qualified financial advisor could be a worthwhile option.
- **Focus on Long-Term Goals:** As a young entrepreneur with a long time horizon, you have the advantage of time in your favor. Don't get discouraged by short-term market fluctuations. Focus on investing for the long term and remain patient. The power of compound interest (interest earned on both the initial investment and accumulated interest) can work wonders over time, allowing your investments to grow significantly.

Additional Resources for Young Investors

Here are some helpful resources to get you started on your investment journey:

- **The U.S. Securities and Exchange Commission (SEC):** https://www.sec.gov/ offers a wealth of information for investors, including resources specifically geared towards young people.
- **The Investor.gov:** https://www.investor.gov/ is a government website providing unbiased information about investing basics and different investment options.
- **Financial Literacy and Education Commission:** https://www.mymoney.gov/ offers educational resources and tools to help young people develop sound financial habits.
- **Online Investment Platforms:** Many online investment platforms cater to young investors, offering user-friendly interfaces, educational resources, and commission-free trades (meaning you don't pay a fee every time you buy or sell an investment). Carefully research different platforms before choosing one, considering factors like fees, investment options available, account minimums, and educational resources offered.

Investing is a marathon, not a sprint. Taking a thoughtful, informed approach, starting early, and focusing on your long-term goals, will enable you to be able to leverage the power of investing to build a secure financial future and achieve true financial self-sufficiency as a young entrepreneur.

MAKING SMART MONEY DECISIONS

Now that you're generating profits, it's natural to wonder how to manage your newfound wealth effectively. Making smart money decisions is crucial for any entrepreneur, but especially for young ones like yourself.

Building a Strong Financial Foundation

Before diving into specific financial strategies, let's establish a solid foundation. Here are some key principles to keep in mind:

- **Developing a Healthy Financial Mindset:** A healthy financial mindset is the cornerstone of smart money management. It involves understanding the value of money, setting realistic financial goals, and prioritizing responsible spending habits. Challenge yourself to think critically about your purchases. Ask yourself if something is a "want" or a true "need" for your business or personal life. Don't fall prey to impulse purchases or keep up with the Joneses. Instead, focus on delayed gratification and prioritize saving and investing for your future.
- **Tracking Your Income and Expenses:** Knowledge is power, especially when it comes to your finances. Develop a system for tracking your income (money coming in) and expenses (money going out). There are many budgeting apps and online tools available to help you categorize your spending. Popular options include Mint, YNAB (You Need a Budget), and Personal Capital. These tools allow you to categorize your spending (rent, groceries, business supplies, marketing costs), identify areas for improvement, and gain valuable insights into your financial habits. Regularly review your income and expenses to see where your money is going and identify areas where you can cut back or optimize spending.

- **Creating a Budget:** A budget is your roadmap to financial success. It outlines how you plan to allocate your income towards various expenses (business costs, personal needs, savings, etc.). There are different budgeting methods to choose from, like the 50/30/20 rule (allocating 50% of your income to needs like rent, groceries, and utilities, 30% to wants like entertainment and dining out, and 20% to savings and debt repayment). Another popular method is the zero-based budget, where you assign every dollar of income to a specific expense category until your income and expenses balance out to zero. Find a system that works best for you and stick to it as much as possible. Review and adjust your budget regularly to reflect changes in your income or business needs.

Separating Business and Personal Finances

As a young entrepreneur, it's crucial to maintain clear boundaries between your business and personal finances. Here's why:

- **Clarity and Organization:** Keeping separate accounts makes it easier to track your business performance. You'll be able to identify profitable ventures, calculate your true business profit, and manage tax filing more efficiently. Expenses related to your business (supplies, marketing materials, software subscriptions) should be paid for from your business account. Treat any profits you generate from your business venture as income, not personal funds to freely spend. Commingling funds can make it difficult to understand your business's financial health and profitability.
- **Liability Protection:** Mingling business and personal finances can expose you to greater risks. If your business faces a lawsuit or encounters financial

difficulties, your personal assets (car, savings) might be at stake if you haven't established proper separation. Depending on your business structure (sole proprietorship, partnership, LLC), consult with a financial advisor or legal professional to understand the best practices for separating your finances. An LLC (Limited Liability Company) can offer some liability protection, shielding your personal assets from business debts and lawsuits. However, it's important to note that even with an LLC, there might be situations where personal assets could be at risk.

Saving for Your Future

Building a savings habit is essential for any aspiring entrepreneur. Here are a few saving strategies to consider:

- **Emergency Fund:** Life throws curveballs. Set aside a safety net to cover unexpected expenses, like equipment repairs or business fluctuations. Aim to save 3-6 months' worth of your business operating costs in a high-yield savings account. This emergency fund will provide peace of mind and prevent you from dipping into personal savings or accumulating debt in case of unforeseen circumstances. Having a separate emergency fund for your business helps maintain a clear separation between your personal finances and business finances.
- **Saving for Specific Business Goals:** In addition to an emergency fund, consider saving toward specific business goals. This could be anything from purchasing new equipment to expanding your marketing reach. Set clear goals and designate specific savings accounts for each goal. Track your progress and adjust your savings strategy as needed. For example, if you're aiming to save for a new laptop essential for your business operations, consider setting up a separate

savings account and allocating a portion of your profits each month to reach your target amount within a specific timeframe.

- **Investing for Long-Term Growth:** While saving is crucial, consider investing a portion of your profits for long-term growth. Investing allows your money to work for you over time through interest, dividends, or capital appreciation (increase in share price). Explore various investment options suitable for young investors, keeping in mind your risk tolerance and financial goals. Here are a few options to consider:
    - **High-Yield Savings Accounts:** These accounts offer a slightly higher interest rate compared to traditional savings accounts. While still considered low-risk, they can help your money grow a little faster than inflation, preserving its purchasing power over time. Look for accounts with minimal fees and easy access to your funds for short-term needs or emergencies. These accounts can be a good option for your business emergency fund or for saving towards short-term business goals.
    - **Certificates of Deposit (CDs):** CDs offer a fixed interest rate for a predetermined period (typically ranging from a few months to several years). They are a good option for a specific long-term goal (think college tuition or a major business investment down the line) if you can commit to not needing the money before the CD matures. Early withdrawal often comes with penalties that eat into your potential earnings. Shop around for CDs with competitive interest rates and terms that align with your goals. Consider a "laddered CD" strategy, where you invest in CDs with different maturity dates to ensure regular access to a portion of your

savings while still benefiting from the potential for higher interest rates on longer-term CDs.

- **Fractional Shares:** The rise of fractional share investing platforms has opened doors for young investors. These platforms allow you to purchase a fraction of a share in a publicly traded company, making it possible to invest in high-priced stocks that might have been out of reach otherwise. Fractional shares offer diversification and the potential for growth, but Remember that the stock market is inherently risky. Stock prices can fluctuate significantly, and you could potentially lose money on your investment. Do your research on companies before investing in their fractional shares, focusing on their financial health, industry trends, and long-term growth prospects.

Making Informed Purchases

As a business owner, every purchase decision should be carefully considered. Here are some tips for making smart spending choices:

- **Value vs. Price:** Don't always be swayed by the lowest price tag. Research different options and prioritize quality and long-term value. A seemingly cheaper product might require frequent replacements, ultimately costing you more in the long run. Look for products with good warranties and customer reviews. Consider the total cost of ownership, factoring in potential maintenance or repair costs associated with a product.
- **Return on Investment (ROI):** Evaluate potential investments (equipment, software, marketing campaigns) in terms of their potential return on investment. Consider how a purchase will contribute to

your business growth, increase productivity, or generate additional revenue. Focus on investments that have the potential to pay for themselves and contribute to your overall business goals. For example, if you're considering investing in marketing software, calculate the potential increase in sales generated by the software compared to the cost of the software itself.

- **Cost-Benefit Analysis:** Before making a major purchase, conduct a cost-benefit analysis. This involves weighing the potential benefits of a purchase against its associated costs. Consider not just the initial cost, but also ongoing expenses like maintenance, subscriptions, or additional resources required to operate the equipment or software. Evaluate if the benefits outweigh the costs and if the purchase aligns with your overall business strategy.

Building Credit for the Future

Establishing good credit is essential for any entrepreneur. Here are some tips for responsible borrowing:

- **Understanding Credit:** Credit refers to your ability to borrow money and repay it on time. A good credit score allows you to secure loans for future business endeavors, potentially with lower interest rates. There are two main credit bureaus: Experian, Equifax, and TransUnion. You can obtain a free credit report from each bureau annually to monitor your credit score and ensure there are no errors.
- **Building Credit History:** If you don't have any credit history yet, consider applying for a secured credit card. With a secured credit card, you make a deposit that serves as your credit limit. Using the card responsibly and making timely payments can help build your credit score.

- **Borrowing Responsibly:** Only borrow what you can afford to repay. Avoid accumulating high-interest debt that can cripple your business financially. Before taking out a loan, create a solid business plan and calculate how you'll use the loan funds to generate revenue and repay the debt. Shop around for lenders and compare interest rates, repayment terms, and any associated fees.

- **Managing Credit Wisely:** Once you have access to credit, use it wisely and make payments on time. Late payments can significantly damage your credit score. Set up automatic payments to avoid missed due dates. Maintain a low credit utilization ratio (the amount of credit you're using compared to your total credit limit). A lower ratio indicates responsible credit management and can positively impact your credit score.

Insurance Considerations

As your business grows, consider investing in appropriate insurance coverage to protect yourself from unforeseen circumstances. Here are some types of insurance to consider:

- **General Liability Insurance:** This type of insurance protects your business from lawsuits arising from property damage, bodily injury, or personal injury caused by your business operations.
- **Business Property Insurance:** This insurance covers damage or loss to your business property (equipment, inventory) due to events like fire, theft, or vandalism.
- **Business Interruption Insurance:** This insurance reimburses you for lost income if your business is forced to temporarily close due to a covered event.

Consult with a qualified insurance broker to assess your specific business needs and recommend the most appropriate insurance coverage.

Seeking Professional Guidance:

Managing your finances as a young entrepreneur can be challenging. Don't hesitate to seek professional guidance when needed. Here are some resources available to you:

- **Financial Advisors:** A financial advisor can provide personalized advice on your financial goals, including saving, investing, and managing your business finances. Look for advisors who specialize in working with young entrepreneurs.
- **Mentorship Programs:** Many organizations offer mentorship programs that connect young entrepreneurs with experienced business professionals. Mentors can provide valuable guidance and support on financial management and other aspects of running a successful business.
- **Online Resources:** There are numerous online resources available to help young people learn about personal finance and business management. These resources can provide valuable information on topics such as budgeting, investing, taxes, and business planning.

The earlier you start learning and making responsible financial choices, the better equipped you'll be to navigate the world of business and achieve your entrepreneurial dreams.

CHAPTER 7

THE JOURNEY CONTINUES

OVERCOMING CHALLENGES AND ADAPTING TO CHANGE

Congratulations on launching your teen business! You've taken a brave step towards financial self-sufficiency, and the journey ahead is sure to be filled with exciting opportunities and rewarding experiences. However, the road to success is rarely smooth. As a young entrepreneur, you'll inevitably encounter challenges and unexpected turns.

Common Challenges Faced by Teen Businesses

While every business is unique, some challenges are common for teen entrepreneurs. Here's a glimpse of what you might face:

- **Limited Resources:** As a teen, your access to capital, time, and experienced personnel might be limited. Starting small and bootstrapping your business (funding it with your own resources) is likely the initial approach. Here are some strategies to navigate these limitations:
    - **Resourcefulness is Key:** Explore cost-effective marketing strategies. Utilize free or low-cost online tools for website creation, graphic design, and social media management. Barter your skills or services with other young entrepreneurs to gain access to resources you might not have the budget for initially. Consider crowdfunding platforms to raise capital for specific business goals, but ensure you have a well-defined campaign and realistic fundraising target.

  - **Time Management is Crucial:** Create a schedule that prioritizes both your business and your personal commitments. Utilize time management techniques like the Pomodoro Technique (working in focused 25-minute intervals with short breaks) to maximize productivity during your dedicated business working hours. Delegate tasks when possible, especially as your business grows. Consider collaborating with friends or classmates who share your entrepreneurial spirit, leveraging their skillsets to distribute workload and responsibilities.
- **Balancing Business and Life:** Juggling schoolwork, extracurricular activities, and a budding business can be demanding. Here are some tips to maintain a healthy balance:
  - **Set Realistic Expectations:** Don't expect to become an overnight success. Building a successful business takes time and dedication. Set realistic goals for yourself and your business, acknowledging the limitations on your time as a busy teenager. Celebrate small wins and milestones along the way to stay motivated.
  - **Prioritize Communication:** Communicate openly with your teachers, parents, and friends about your business commitments. Explain your workload and schedule adjustments, and seek their understanding and support. Negotiate flexible deadlines or alternative arrangements for schoolwork if necessary.
- **Market Saturation and Competition:** Your chosen niche might already have established competitors. Here are some ways to stand out:
  - **Conduct Thorough Market Research:** Understand your target audience and identify any gaps in the market your business can fill.

Analyze existing competitors, their strengths and weaknesses, and what makes them successful. Identify a unique selling proposition (USP) for your business, whether it's a specific product line, exceptional customer service, a strong focus on local sourcing, or a commitment to sustainability.

  - **Build a Strong Brand Identity:** Develop a clear and consistent brand identity that reflects your values and resonates with your target audience. This includes your logo, visual design elements, brand messaging, and overall customer experience.
  - **Leverage Social Media Effectively:** Utilize social media platforms to connect with your target audience, showcase your products or services, and build a loyal customer base. Run engaging content campaigns, participate in relevant online communities, and utilize targeted social media advertising to reach your ideal customers. Consider partnering with relevant social media influencers to promote your brand to their audience.

- **Marketing and Customer Acquisition:** Reaching your target audience and attracting customers can be a challenge, especially with limited marketing budgets. Here are some cost-effective strategies:
  - **Content Marketing:** Create valuable and informative content (blog posts, social media posts, videos) relevant to your target audience. This establishes you as an expert in your field and attracts customers searching for information and solutions related to your products or services.
  - **Public Relations (PR):** Pitch local newspapers, magazines, or online publications about your business story. Offer to be

interviewed as an expert in your niche, or provide guest articles. Getting media coverage can significantly increase brand awareness and attract new customers without a significant financial investment.

  - **Networking and Building Partnerships:** Connect with other young entrepreneurs and local businesses in your community. Explore opportunities for collaboration, joint marketing initiatives, or cross-promotion. Participating in local events or farmers markets can also be a great way to reach new customers and network with potential partners.

- **Legal and Regulatory Considerations:** Depending on your business model and location, there might be legal and regulatory requirements you need to comply with. Here's how to navigate this:
  - **Research Local Regulations:** Familiar yourself with local business regulations, zoning restrictions, and any necessary permits or licenses. Visit your local government's website or contact your city's business development office for guidance. Resources like the Small Business Administration (SBA) website also offer valuable information on legal requirements for young entrepreneurs.
  - **Consult with a Mentor:** Consider seeking guidance from a business lawyer or mentor familiar with the legalities of operating a business in your area. They can advise you on the appropriate business structure (sole proprietorship, partnership, LLC), tax implications, and any necessary legal documents or contracts you might need.

Developing a Growth Mindset

Challenges are inevitable, but they can also be opportunities for growth. Here's how to cultivate a resilient mindset:

- **Embrace the Learning Curve:** View challenges as learning experiences. Analyze each obstacle and identify areas for improvement. For example, if a marketing campaign doesn't yield the desired results, analyze the data, understand what went wrong, and refine your strategy for future campaigns. Use these setbacks to refine your business strategy and build a stronger foundation for future success.
- **Develop Problem-Solving Skills:** Don't let setbacks paralyze you. Approach challenges with a problem-solving mentality. Brainstorm solutions with a team of friends or mentors, research potential strategies, and be open to creative approaches. For instance, if you encounter difficulties sourcing materials from a specific supplier, explore alternative suppliers, consider using recycled materials, or potentially adjust your product design to accommodate readily available options.
- **Adapt and Pivot:** The business landscape is constantly evolving. Be prepared to adapt your strategies as needed. Stay informed about industry trends, customer preferences, and technological advancements. Don't be afraid to pivot your business model if necessary to stay relevant and competitive. For example, if you initially launched a brick-and-mortar retail store, but online shopping trends are surging, consider developing a strong e-commerce presence alongside your physical storefront.
- **Celebrate Small Wins:** The road to success is paved with small victories. Acknowledge and celebrate your achievements, no matter how seemingly insignificant. Did you receive your first positive customer review?

Did you successfully complete a complex order fulfillment process? These milestones fuel your motivation and keep you moving forward, especially during challenging times. Celebrating small wins with your team or mentors can also foster a positive and supportive work environment.

Mastering the Art of Adaptation: Strategies for Navigating Change

The business world is dynamic, and change is constant. Here's how to remain adaptable in the face of unexpected developments:

- **Maintaining a Flexible Business Model:** Structure your business with the ability to adapt. Avoid rigid processes that can hinder your ability to respond to change. Consider incorporating modular elements into your business model, allowing for adjustments without having to overhaul your entire system. For instance, if you offer customized products, ensure your production process can accommodate variations in customer requests without significantly impacting lead times or costs.
- **Customer Feedback Loop:** Actively solicit feedback from your customers. Conduct surveys, host focus groups, and engage with your audience on social media. Utilize this feedback to understand their evolving needs and preferences. Refine your product offerings, marketing strategies, and customer service approach based on customer insights. For example, if customer feedback highlights a need for faster shipping options, explore partnerships with new delivery providers or adjust your pricing structure to include expedited shipping options.
- **Embrace New Technologies:** Technology advancements can revolutionize your business. Stay

informed about the latest tools and platforms relevant to your industry. Explore how technology can enhance your operations, improve your marketing reach, or streamline your customer service. For instance, consider utilizing online project management tools to collaborate with remote team members, or explore the use of chatbots to provide 24/7 customer support.

- **Embrace Continuous Learning:** Never stop learning and growing as an entrepreneur. Read industry publications, attend workshops and conferences, and connect with other young business owners. Seek out mentors who can offer valuable insights and guidance. The more you learn, the better equipped you'll be to adapt to change and navigate new challenges. Consider online learning platforms and educational resources specifically designed for young entrepreneurs.

Building a Support System: Resources for Young Entrepreneurs

As a young entrepreneur, having a support system is crucial. Here are some resources available to you:

- **Mentorship Programs:** Many organizations offer mentorship programs that connect young entrepreneurs with experienced business professionals. Mentors can provide valuable guidance on financial management, marketing strategies, legal considerations, and navigating the challenges of running a business. Look for mentorship programs specifically focused on young entrepreneurs or those catering to your specific industry.
- **Online Communities:** There are numerous online communities and forums dedicated to young entrepreneurs. These platforms provide a space to connect with peers, share experiences, ask questions,

and offer support to one another. Participating in online communities can help you feel less isolated in your entrepreneurial journey and provide access to a wealth of collective knowledge and experience.

- **Local Business Development Centers (SBDCs):** The Small Business Administration (SBA) network of SBDCs offers free or low-cost business counseling and educational resources for aspiring entrepreneurs. SBDC advisors can provide valuable guidance on topics like business plan development, marketing strategies, legal compliance, and accessing funding.
- **Young Entrepreneur Competitions:** Many organizations host competitions specifically for young entrepreneurs. Participating in such competitions can be a great way to gain valuable feedback on your business idea, network with potential investors or mentors, and potentially win prize money or other resources to support your business growth.

The road to building a successful business is rarely smooth. There will be challenges, setbacks, and unexpected turns. However, by cultivating resilience, embracing adaptability, and building a strong support system, you can overcome these hurdles and navigate change effectively. Success doesn't happen overnight. Be patient, stay focused on your goals, and never stop learning.

SCALING UP YOUR BUSINESS FOR FUTURE SUCCESS

After having launched your teen business, weathered initial challenges, and established a solid foundation. Now, the entrepreneurial spirit within you might be yearning for more – growth and expansion.

Scaling vs. Stagnation

Before diving into specific strategies, it's crucial to differentiate between scaling and stagnation. Scaling refers to intentionally expanding your business operations to reach new heights. Stagnation, on the other hand, is remaining stagnant, maintaining your current level of operation without significant growth.

Scaling offers numerous benefits:

- **Increased Revenue and Profit:** Reaching a wider audience and selling more products or services translates to increased revenue and potential for higher profits. You'll be able to reinvest these profits back into your business for further growth, potentially allowing you to hire additional staff, invest in research and development, or expand your product line.
- **Enhanced Brand Recognition:** As your business grows, so does your brand awareness. A well-recognized brand attracts more customers and fosters customer loyalty. Customers are more likely to choose a familiar brand they trust, especially in a crowded marketplace.
- **Improved Efficiency and Economies of Scale:** Scaling often allows you to streamline operations and leverage economies of scale. This can involve bulk purchasing of materials at lower costs, negotiating better deals with suppliers, or implementing automated processes to increase efficiency. For example, if you create handcrafted jewelry, scaling your business might allow you to purchase beads and other materials in bulk at a discounted rate, significantly reducing your production costs.
- **Attracting Talent and Investment:** A growing business becomes more attractive to potential employees and investors. This can help you attract top

talent to your team and secure funding for further expansion. A talented and experienced team can bring valuable expertise and fresh perspectives to your business, while securing investment can provide the resources needed to accelerate your growth plans.

However, scaling also comes with challenges:

- **Maintaining Quality Control:** As your business grows, ensuring consistent quality across your products or services becomes crucial. Establish clear quality control procedures to avoid compromising your brand reputation. This might involve implementing standardized production processes, conducting thorough quality checks at different stages of production, or gathering customer feedback to identify areas for improvement.
- **Managing Increased Complexity:** A larger business involves more complex operations, inventory management, and potentially a larger team. Developing strong organizational skills and leadership qualities will be essential. You might need to implement new systems and processes to manage a larger inventory, delegate tasks effectively to your team, and track your business performance across different metrics.
- **Adapting to New Challenges:** Scaling introduces new challenges, such as managing a larger workforce, navigating legal and regulatory complexities, and potentially entering new markets. Be prepared to adapt your business model, marketing strategies, and overall operations as your business grows. Staying informed about industry trends, legal requirements, and potential risks will be crucial for navigating these challenges effectively.

Scaling Strategies

Now that you understand the difference between scaling and stagnation, let's explore specific strategies to propel your teen business forward:

- **Market Research and Expansion:**
  - **Identify Growth Opportunities:** Conduct thorough market research to identify potential growth opportunities. Is there a demand for your products or services in new geographical locations? Could you expand your product line to cater to a broader customer base? For instance, if you create custom-designed t-shirts, market research might reveal a high demand for eco-friendly clothing. You could then explore offering t-shirts made from organic cotton or recycled materials to cater to a growing environmentally conscious customer segment.
  - **Refine Your Target Audience:** As you scale, consider refining your target audience. A broader audience might require adjustments to your marketing message or product offerings to resonate effectively. For example, if you initially targeted children with your custom t-shirt business, scaling might involve expanding your target audience to include teenagers and young adults. This could involve offering a wider range of designs and styles that appeal to a broader age group.
  - **Develop a Growth Strategy:** Based on your market research, create a well-defined growth strategy. This might involve entering new markets online or offline, launching new product lines, or offering additional services to your existing customer base. For instance, your growth strategy could involve setting up an

online store to reach a wider audience or developing a subscription box service where customers receive a new custom-designed t-shirt every month.

- **Optimizing Operations for Efficiency:**
  - **Streamline Processes:** Analyze your current operations and identify areas for improvement. Can you automate certain tasks, such as order processing or inventory management? Can you implement more efficient workflow management systems? Streamlining processes can free up valuable time and resources for growth initiatives. For example, if you currently manage customer orders and inventory manually through spreadsheets, scaling your business might necessitate implementing an inventory management software that automates stock tracking and order fulfillment.
  - **Leverage Technology:** Explore how technology can enhance your operations. Utilize project management software like Asana or Trello to manage tasks and deadlines for your team. Implement customer relationship management (CRM) tools like Salesforce or HubSpot to track customer interactions and build stronger customer relationships. Explore online accounting platforms like Xero or Quickbooks to streamline your financial management and gain valuable insights into your business performance.
  - **Outsource When Necessary:** Don't be afraid to outsource tasks that can be handled more efficiently by external specialists. This allows you to focus on your core competencies and strategic decision-making. For example, consider outsourcing your social media management to a marketing agency specializing

in social media marketing for young businesses. This allows you to leverage their expertise and free up your time to focus on product development or customer service.

- **Building a Strong Team:**
    - **Identify Skill Gaps:** As your business grows, your skillset needs might evolve. Identify any skill gaps within your team and consider hiring new team members to fill those gaps. For instance, if you initially focused on the creative aspects of your t-shirt business, scaling might require hiring someone with experience in marketing and e-commerce to manage your online store and marketing campaigns.
    - **Delegate Effectively:** Delegation is crucial for scaling a business. Empower your team members to take ownership of tasks and projects. Provide clear instructions, set deadlines, and offer ongoing support to ensure successful task completion. Utilize performance reviews to provide constructive feedback and identify areas for growth within your team.
    - **Invest in Team Development:** Investing in your team's professional development is crucial for long-term success. Encourage your team members to attend workshops, conferences, or online courses relevant to their roles. Provide opportunities for mentorship within your team or with experienced entrepreneurs in your community. A well-trained and motivated team is essential for scaling your business effectively.
- **Marketing and Customer Acquisition Strategies:**
    - **Refine Your Marketing Message:** As you refine your target audience and potentially enter new markets, your marketing message might

need adjustments. Ensure your message resonates with your ideal customer and clearly communicates the value proposition of your products or services. For instance, if you're expanding your t-shirt business to target teenagers, your marketing message might shift to emphasize the trendy and customizable designs that appeal to this demographic.

- **Expand Your Marketing Reach:** Explore new marketing channels to reach a wider audience. Consider utilizing social media advertising platforms like Facebook Ads or Instagram Ads to target your ideal customers based on demographics, interests, and online behavior. Explore influencer marketing by partnering with social media personalities relevant to your target audience to promote your products or services. Content marketing strategies like creating blog posts or videos showcasing your design process or highlighting customer stories can also be effective in attracting new customers.
- **Develop a Customer Retention Strategy:** Acquiring new customers is important, but retaining existing customers is equally crucial. Develop a customer retention strategy that fosters loyalty and encourages repeat business. Offer loyalty programs or exclusive discounts to reward your existing customer base. Solicit customer feedback through surveys or email campaigns to understand their needs and preferences, and continuously strive to improve your products or services based on their input.

- **Financial Planning and Investment:**
    - **Develop a Financial Forecast:** As you scale your business, creating a financial forecast becomes increasingly important. This forecast

should project your future revenue, expenses, and potential profits based on your growth strategy. A financial forecast helps you make informed decisions about resource allocation, investment needs, and potential risks associated with your expansion plans.

- **Secure Funding:** Scaling your business might require additional funding. Explore various funding options, such as personal savings, small business loans, or angel investors. Carefully evaluate the terms and conditions of any loans or investments before accepting them. Consider pitching your business idea to angel investors or venture capitalists if your growth strategy requires significant upfront investment. Be prepared to present a compelling business plan that outlines your vision, growth strategy, and financial projections.
- **Manage Your Cash Flow Effectively:** Managing your cash flow effectively is crucial for the financial health of your growing business. Develop a system for tracking your income and expenses, and ensure you have sufficient cash reserves to cover operational costs and unexpected expenses. Consider implementing invoicing and payment processing systems that allow you to collect payments from customers efficiently.

Scaling your teen business is an exciting journey filled with challenges and rewards. By understanding the difference between scaling and stagnation, developing a well-defined growth strategy, and implementing the strategies outlined in this chapter, you can transform your teen venture into a sustainable and scalable business. Remember that the key to successful scaling lies in:

- **Maintaining a Customer-Centric Approach:** Never lose sight of your customers. Focus on delivering exceptional customer service, consistently exceeding their expectations. Gather customer feedback regularly and use it to refine your products or services to better serve their evolving needs.
- **Adaptability and Continuous Learning:** The business landscape is constantly evolving. Be prepared to adapt your strategies based on changing market trends, customer preferences, and technological advancements. Embrace continuous learning, attend workshops and conferences relevant to your industry, and stay informed about industry best practices.
- **Building a Strong Support Network:** Surround yourself with a supportive network of mentors, advisors, and fellow young entrepreneurs. This network can provide valuable guidance, resources, and mentorship as you navigate the challenges of scaling your business.

The journey from a small seed of an idea to a towering redwood of a business takes time, dedication, and a willingness to learn and grow. Embrace the challenges, celebrate your successes, and enjoy the empowering journey of scaling your teen business into a thriving enterprise.

BUILDING A STRONG WORK-LIFE BALANCE

This is one area I wish I had someone to give me advice on when I was younger. I did so much of work, both as an employee and as an entrepreneur when I was younger that I ended up having no time for anything else. Little to no time for my academics, my friends, my family, my faith, and even myself. While the drive to succeed is commendable, navigating the world of business as a teenager requires a crucial skill – building a strong work-life balance. This ensures that you don't experience burn-out or start sidelining other very important parts of your life.

Understanding the Importance of Balance

Why is work-life balance important, especially for a busy teen entrepreneur? Here's why:

- **Maintaining Well-being:** A healthy balance between work and personal life reduces stress, promotes better sleep, and allows you to recharge. This translates to increased focus, improved decision-making abilities, and ultimately, better performance in both your business and personal endeavors. Studies by the American Psychological Association highlight the negative impact of chronic stress on cognitive function, memory, and creativity – all essential skills for a successful entrepreneur.
- **Prioritizing Education:** As a teenager, education remains paramount. A healthy work-life balance ensures you have dedicated time to studies, homework, and extracurricular activities that contribute to your overall intellectual and social development. Research by the National Bureau of Economic Research suggests that strong academic performance can lead to greater business success later in life.
- **Maintaining Relationships:** Building strong relationships with family and friends provides emotional support and a sense of belonging. A balanced approach allows you to nurture these relationships and avoid neglecting the people who matter to you. Strong social connections have been shown to reduce stress and increase feelings of happiness, both of which can benefit your overall well-being and entrepreneurial drive.
- **Preventing Burnout:** Pushing yourself too hard without adequate rest or relaxation can lead to burnout

– a state of emotional, physical, and mental exhaustion. Maintaining a balanced schedule helps you avoid burnout and maintain the motivation and energy needed for long-term success. Studies by the Mayo Clinic indicate that burnout can lead to feelings of cynicism, detachment, and reduced productivity – all detrimental to your business endeavors.

Challenges to Work-Life Balance

Balancing business pursuits with a busy teenage life comes with its own set of challenges:

- **Time Management:** Juggling school, extracurricular activities, chores, and business obligations can be overwhelming. Effective time management skills are crucial for carving out dedicated time for each essential aspect of your life. The constant pressure to "be on" and available can lead to a feeling of being stretched too thin.
- **Passion and Drive:** The passion for your business venture can be a double-edged sword. While it fuels your drive, it can also lead to neglecting other responsibilities if left unchecked. The constant "hustle" mentality glorified in some entrepreneurial circles can create unrealistic expectations and lead to sacrificing personal well-being for short-term gains.
- **Parental Expectations:** Parents might have concerns about your business venture impacting your academic performance or overall well-being. Their anxieties may stem from a lack of understanding about the business world or a fear of you neglecting your studies. Communication is key to alleviating these concerns.
- **Peer Pressure and Social Comparison:** Seeing peers engage in social activities while you're focused on business tasks might trigger feelings of isolation or

missing out (FOMO). The pressure to conform to social norms and participate in every activity can create internal conflict.

- **Technological Distractions:** The constant presence of smartphones and social media can be a major time drain and hinder your ability to focus on tasks. The fear of missing out on online communication can lead to fragmented attention and decreased productivity.

Strategies for Building a Balanced Life

Now that you understand the importance and challenges of work-life balance, let's explore strategies to achieve it:

- **Prioritization and Time Management:**
    - **Create a Schedule:** Develop a weekly or monthly schedule that clearly outlines time slots for schoolwork, business tasks, chores, personal time, and sleep. Blocking specific time slots for each activity ensures you dedicate focused attention to each area. Utilize tools like calendar apps or planners to visually represent your schedule and track your progress.
    - **Prioritize Relentlessly:** Not all tasks are created equal. Learn to differentiate between urgent and important tasks. Utilize tools like the Eisenhower Matrix to categorize tasks based on urgency and importance, helping you focus on high-priority business tasks first. Urgent tasks require immediate attention, while important tasks contribute to your long-term goals.
    - **Delegate and Outsource:** Don't be afraid to delegate tasks within your business to family members or friends who can offer help. Consider outsourcing specific tasks, like social media management or graphic design, if your budget allows. Delegation and outsourcing free

up valuable time for you to focus on essential tasks and personal commitments.

- **Maintaining Healthy Habits:**
  - **Prioritize Sleep:** Aim for 7-8 hours of quality sleep each night. Adequate sleep improves concentration, memory, and decision-making abilities, all of which are crucial for your business endeavors and academic performance. Develop a consistent sleep schedule and create a relaxing bedtime routine to ensure restful sleep.
  - **Maintain a Healthy Diet:** Fuel your body with nutritious foods to maintain energy levels throughout the day. Plan your meals and snacks in advance to avoid unhealthy options when pressed for time. Pack healthy snacks for school or during business errands to avoid relying on vending machines or fast food. Focus on incorporating fruits, vegetables, whole grains, and lean protein sources into your diet.
  - **Schedule Physical Activity:** Integrate regular physical activity into your routine. Exercise releases endorphins, improves mood, and reduces stress, contributing to overall well-being and productivity. Aim for at least 30 minutes of moderate-intensity exercise most days of the week. Choose activities you enjoy, such as running, swimming, team sports, or dancing.
  - **Practice Relaxation Techniques:** Learn relaxation techniques like deep breathing or meditation to manage stress and maintain mental clarity. Taking short breaks throughout the day to practice these techniques can help you return to your tasks feeling refreshed and

focused. Consider mindfulness exercises or yoga to cultivate a sense of calm and inner peace.

- **Communication and Setting Boundaries:**
    - **Communicate with Parents and Teachers:** Open communication with parents and teachers is crucial. Discuss your business commitments and explain how you are managing your time effectively. Demonstrate your ability to prioritize academics and responsibilities. Regular communication fosters trust and understanding, earning their support for your entrepreneurial endeavors.
    - **Set Boundaries with Friends:** Communicate your business commitments to friends and explain when you might be unavailable. Suggest alternative times to hang out or schedule social activities in advance. Be upfront about your need for dedicated work time, but also prioritize spending quality time with friends to maintain healthy social connections.
    - **Embrace the Power of "No":** Learning to say "no" politely but firmly is essential. Don't be afraid to decline additional commitments if your schedule is already full. Prioritize your well-being and focus on tasks that truly add value to your business or personal life.
- **Leveraging Technology for Efficiency:**
    - **Utilize Time Management Apps:** Explore time management apps like Todoist or Trello to create to-do lists, set deadlines, and track your progress on both business and personal tasks. These tools can help you visualize your workload and ensure you're staying on track.
    - **Utilize Productivity Tools:** Take advantage of productivity tools like Grammarly for proofreading, Canva for graphic design, or

scheduling software like Calendly to streamline communication and appointments. These tools can save you valuable time and allow you to focus on more strategic business aspects.

- **Schedule Digital Detox Breaks:** Plan regular breaks from technology throughout the day. Turn off notifications and silence your phone during dedicated work time or while spending time with family and friends. This allows you to focus on the present moment and avoids the constant distraction of social media or email alerts.

Building a strong work-life balance is an ongoing process. There will be days when achieving perfect balance feels impossible. The key is to strive for progress, not perfection. The journey to becoming a successful entrepreneur requires dedication, passion, and a healthy dose of self-care. Embrace the challenges, celebrate your accomplishments, and enjoy the process of building your business alongside a balanced and enriching teenage experience.

CHAPTER 8

YOUR IMPACT ON THE WORLD

INTEGRATING SOCIAL RESPONSIBILITY INTO YOUR BUSINESS

As your venture flourishes, you might be considering ways to expand your impact beyond financial success. Integrating social responsibility into your business practices allows you to contribute positively to your community and the environment, while potentially attracting a loyal customer base that values ethical practices.

Understanding Social Responsibility

Corporate Social Responsibility (CSR) refers to a company's commitment to operating in an ethical and sustainable manner, considering the social and environmental impact of its business decisions. As a teen entrepreneur, integrating social responsibility into your business means going beyond just generating profits. It involves:

- **Ethical Labor Practices:** Ensuring fair wages, safe working conditions, and responsible treatment of employees, regardless of their age or experience level. This includes adhering to labor laws, providing opportunities for professional development, and fostering a positive and inclusive work environment.
- **Environmental Sustainability:** Minimizing your business's environmental footprint through practices like reducing waste, using eco-friendly materials, and conserving energy. Consider your supply chain, packaging choices, and energy consumption to identify areas for improvement.

- **Community Engagement:** Supporting local causes, volunteering your time or skills, or donating to charities that align with your business values. This demonstrates your commitment to the community and allows you to make a positive impact beyond your sales.
- **Transparency and Accountability:** Being open and honest about your business practices and the impact you have on society and the environment. This includes communicating your CSR efforts to your customers and stakeholders, and being receptive to feedback and suggestions for improvement.

Why Integrate Social Responsibility?

There are several compelling reasons to embrace social responsibility as a teen entrepreneur:

- **Attract Customers Who Share Your Values:** Today's consumers, especially younger generations, are increasingly conscious of social and environmental issues. They are more likely to support businesses that align with their values. Demonstrating social responsibility can attract a loyal customer base who appreciate your commitment to making a positive impact. A 2021 Nielsen study found that 66% of global consumers are willing to pay more for sustainable brands.
- **Boost Brand Reputation:** Integrating social responsibility can enhance your brand image and reputation. Customers are more likely to trust and advocate for businesses perceived as ethical and socially conscious. A strong brand reputation can attract new customers, investors, and potential partners.
- **Boost Employee Morale:** Employees who feel their work contributes to a positive social or environmental cause tend to be more engaged and motivated. This can

lead to increased productivity and a lower employee turnover rate in your teen business. Studies by Cone Communications suggest that employees are more likely to stay with a company that demonstrates a strong commitment to CSR.

- **Future-Proof Your Business:** Sustainable practices and ethical operations are becoming increasingly important for businesses of all sizes. Integrating social responsibility now positions your business for long-term success in a world that prioritizes environmental and social well-being. Consumers are increasingly demanding sustainable practices, and regulations are evolving to reflect this shift.
- **Personal Growth and Satisfaction:** Contributing positively to your community and the environment can be a personally rewarding experience. As a young entrepreneur, integrating social responsibility allows you to align your business goals with your desire to make a positive difference in the world. This sense of purpose can be a powerful motivator and source of satisfaction.

Putting Social Responsibility into Practice

Here are some practical strategies you can implement to make your teen business more socially responsible, categorized by the core aspects of CSR:

Ethical Labor Practices:

- **Fair Wages and Benefits:** Even as a teen entrepreneur with limited resources, strive to offer fair wages that are competitive with the local market for similar roles. Consider offering flexible scheduling options that cater to the needs of your teen workforce.

- **Safe Working Conditions:** Ensure your workplace is safe and hazard-free, regardless of its size or location. This could involve implementing safety protocols relevant to your industry, providing necessary equipment, and offering training on safety procedures.
- **Respectful and Inclusive Workplace:** Foster a positive and inclusive work environment where everyone feels valued and respected. This involves promoting diversity and inclusion in your hiring practices and creating a culture of open communication and collaboration.

Environmental Sustainability:

- **Reduce, Reuse, Recycle:** Implement a waste reduction plan in your business. This could involve minimizing packaging materials, using recycled or recyclable materials whenever possible, and exploring ways to reuse or repurpose materials in your production process.
- **Energy Conservation:** Evaluate your business's energy consumption and explore ways to conserve energy. Consider using energy-efficient lighting and appliances, implementing "green" office practices like turning off electronics when not in use, and exploring renewable energy options if feasible.

- **Sustainable Sourcing:** When sourcing materials or products for your business, prioritize suppliers with a commitment to sustainability. Research their manufacturing processes and environmental practices to ensure they align with your values. Look for suppliers who use recycled materials, minimize waste in their production, and prioritize energy efficiency.
- **Minimize Transportation Footprint:** Consider ways to reduce the environmental impact of your

business's transportation needs. This could involve offering local delivery options by bike or using electric vehicles, encouraging customers to pick up products locally, or exploring ways to source materials closer to your production location.

Community Engagement:

- **Volunteer Your Time and Skills:** Organize volunteer events for your employees or partner with local charities for volunteering opportunities. This allows you to give back to your community while fostering team spirit and employee engagement.
- **Support Local Causes:** Donate a portion of your profits to local charities that align with your business values. You could also host fundraising events or offer special products or services where part of the proceeds go to charity.
- **Become a Local Advocate:** Use your platform to raise awareness about important social or environmental issues in your community. This could involve partnering with local organizations, sharing information on social media, or organizing educational events.
- **Support Fair Trade Practices:** If your business involves selling products made by others, consider sourcing them from fair trade organizations. Fair trade ensures that producers receive fair wages and work in safe conditions.

Transparency and Accountability:

- **Develop a CSR Mission Statement:** Articulate your commitment to social responsibility by crafting a clear and concise mission statement that outlines your values and goals. This statement should guide your business practices and inform your stakeholders.

- **Communicate Your Efforts:** Be open and transparent about your social responsibility efforts. Share your CSR initiatives on your website, social media platforms, and marketing materials. This allows customers to understand your commitment and hold you accountable.
- **Gather Feedback and Improve:** Actively seek feedback from customers, employees, and stakeholders on your social responsibility efforts. This feedback can help you identify areas for improvement and ensure your CSR initiatives are meaningful and impactful.

Building a Sustainable Impact

As a teen entrepreneur, you might have limited resources at your disposal. Don't let this deter you from integrating social responsibility into your business. Start by focusing on small, achievable actions that can make a positive impact. As your business grows, you can explore ways to expand your social responsibility efforts and increase your positive impact. Here are some examples of how to start small:

- **Organize a beach clean-up event:** This is a great way to promote environmental awareness and give back to your community. Partner with local environmental organizations for support and guidance.
- **Partner with a local charity:** Offer a discounted product or service to customers who donate to a cause you care about. This allows you to raise awareness for the charity while attracting new customers.
- **Donate a portion of your profits:** Even a small percentage can make a difference for a local charity. Start by dedicating a small portion of your profits to a cause you care about and increase your contribution as your business grows.

- **Implement a "round up" program:** Allow customers to round up their purchase amount to the nearest dollar, with the extra cents being donated to a charity. This is a simple way to engage your customers in your social responsibility efforts.
- **Host a skills-based workshop:** Share your expertise with others by offering a free or low-cost workshop on a topic related to your business. This could be a great way to empower others and contribute to your community's development.

Integrating social responsibility into your teen business allows you to be a force for positive change in the world. By focusing on ethical practices, environmental sustainability, and community engagement, you can build a successful business that makes a meaningful impact.

Remember that even small actions can make a difference, and your commitment to social responsibility can inspire others to do the same. Embrace the opportunity to be a leader in your community and a positive role model for aspiring young entrepreneurs. By combining your entrepreneurial spirit with a sense of social responsibility, you can pave the way for a brighter future for yourself, your community, and the planet.

CONCLUSION

The world of entrepreneurship is no longer reserved for adults. Teenagers, brimming with innovative ideas and boundless energy, are increasingly making their mark on the business landscape. As a conclusion for this book, I will be sharing with you some inspiring stories of real-life teen entrepreneurs who have achieved remarkable success in different walks of life. Their journeys offer valuable insights and serve as a powerful motivator for aspiring young business owners like yourself.

From Hobby to Millions: The Slime Queen

Claire Poche started making slime, a popular squishy toy, as a hobby at the age of 14. Little did she know, her playful creations would transform into a multi-million-dollar business. Claire, with the help of her parents, launched "Claire's Slime Co." in 2016, selling her homemade slime online and at local craft fairs. Recognizing a gap in the market for safe, high-quality slime, Claire used her creativity to develop unique textures, scents, and colors, setting her products apart from the competition. Her dedication and entrepreneurial spirit paid off. "Claire's Slime Co." skyrocketed in popularity, garnering media attention and attracting a massive online following. Today, the company employs several people and offers a wide variety of slime products, apparel, and accessories. Claire's story is a testament to the power of transforming a passion into a successful business venture.

Baking Up a Business: The Teen Chef

At just 12 years old, Isabella Rose Taylor, a self-taught baker, launched "Cookies for Kids Cancer," a non-profit organization dedicated to raising funds for childhood cancer research.

Inspired by her grandmother's battle with cancer, Isabella started baking and selling delicious homemade cookies, donating all proceeds to charity. Her heartfelt initiative quickly captured hearts and imaginations. Local news outlets picked up her story, and soon Isabella was receiving orders from across the country. With support from her family and community, she turned "Cookies for Kids Cancer" into a national phenomenon. The organization has raised millions of dollars for pediatric cancer research and has inspired countless young people to make a difference in their communities. Isabella's story exemplifies the power of combining passion with social responsibility to create a thriving business with a positive impact.

Tech Savvy with a Social Mission: The App Developer

At the age of 15, Nick D'Aloisio developed "Summly," a mobile app that uses artificial intelligence to condense news articles into concise summaries. Nick, fascinated by technology and its potential to improve information access, identified a need for a more efficient way to consume news on smartphones. He spent countless hours coding and refining his app, eventually launching it on the Apple App Store. "Summly" became an instant success, attracting millions of users and capturing the attention of tech giants. Nick's innovative app was acquired by Yahoo! for a staggering $30 million, making him one of the youngest app developers to achieve such a feat. Nick's story highlights the importance of identifying a problem and using technology to develop creative solutions. It also showcases the potential for young entrepreneurs to make a significant impact in the tech sector.

The Power of Social Media: The Teenage Influencer

Building a successful business isn't always about a physical product or service. Teenagers are leveraging the power of social media platforms like Instagram and YouTube to establish themselves as influencers and build brands around their unique personalities and expertise. Makenna Kelly, a 17-year-old fashion enthusiast, started a popular Instagram account where she showcases her personal style and curates fashion inspiration for her followers. Makenna's authenticity and engaging content attracted a loyal following of over a million users. This online audience allowed her to collaborate with major clothing brands and launch her own clothing line. Makenna's story highlights the potential of social media to connect with a global audience and build a successful business as a content creator.

Lessons from Success: Wisdom from Young Entrepreneurs

These are just a few examples of the many inspiring young entrepreneurs who are paving the way for a new generation of business leaders. As you embark on your own entrepreneurial journey, here are some key takeaways from their success stories, which is also a summary of the major talking points that we've discussed during the course of this book:

- **Follow your passion:** The most successful businesses are often built around a genuine passion or interest.
- **Identify a need and fill it:** Look for opportunities to solve problems or fill unmet needs in your community or target market.
- **Embrace innovation:** Think creatively, develop unique solutions, and don't be afraid to challenge the status quo.
- **Leverage technology:** Utilize the power of technology to streamline operations, connect with customers, and build a strong online presence.
- **Build a strong support system:** Surround yourself with mentors, advisors, and family members who believe in your vision and can offer guidance.

- **Be persistent and dedicated:** Building a successful business takes time, hard work, and resilience. Don't be discouraged by setbacks. Learn from your mistakes, adapt your approach, and keep pushing forward.

- **Give back to your community:** Many successful young entrepreneurs like Isabella Rose Taylor use their platforms and resources to make a positive impact on their communities. Consider ways your business can contribute to social causes you care about.
- **Never stop learning:** The world of business is constantly evolving. Stay curious, continue to learn new skills, and adapt to changing market trends.

Beyond Inspiration: Taking Action

The stories of these young trailblazers serve as a powerful motivator, but inspiration alone isn't enough. To achieve your own entrepreneurial dreams, you need to translate that inspiration into action. Here are some practical steps to get you started:

- **Identify your business idea:** Brainstorm ideas based on your interests, skills, and observations of unmet needs in your community.
- **Conduct market research:** Validate your idea by researching your target market, potential competitors, and industry trends.
- **Develop a business plan:** This will outline your business concept, target market, marketing strategy, financial projections, and roadmap for success.
- **Secure funding:** There are various ways to finance your business, including personal savings, loans from family or friends, crowdfunding platforms, or pitch competitions.
- **Choose a business structure:** Decide on a sole proprietorship, partnership, or Limited Liability

Company (LLC) structure based on your business needs and legal requirements.
- **Obtain necessary licenses and permits:** Research the permits and licenses required to operate your business in your location.
- **Market your business:** Develop a marketing strategy to reach your target audience and create brand awareness. Utilize online platforms, social media marketing, or local advertising strategies depending on your business type.
- **Manage your finances:** Keep accurate records of your income and expenses, set realistic budgets, and explore ways to manage your finances effectively.
- **Comply with legal and tax regulations:** Ensure your business complies with all relevant tax regulations and legal requirements.

Launching a successful business is a journey, not a destination. It is no easy task to start up a business, and it is even more difficult to keep it afloat, and much more difficult to elevate it into the profit column. But understand that even if your business fails, the more important thing is that you started something.

Most people go through their entire lives without being able to say that they ever started any kind of money-making venture on their own, and so if you can separate yourself from that crowd, it is a great achievement on its own.

But if your business fails, don't be quick to try and start another one. Take a step back and examine why. The why is much more important than the fact that it failed, because if you can't see why it failed, you won't be able to avoid making the same mistake again, and so your next business would be doomed to fail before it would even start. It's like falling down. When you fall down, you look back and down to see why you fell. If you kicked a stone, you know to either remove the stone or avoid it. If the ground was slippery, you know to clean it up or avoid that area. If you can't find what made you fall, you will most likely fall again. That's the same way it is in business, both for adults and for teens.

There will be challenges and obstacles along the way. Embrace the learning process, be adaptable, and most importantly, never lose sight of your passion and vision. The stories of these young entrepreneurs are a testament to the power of perseverance, creativity, and a strong work ethic. With dedication and the right tools, you too can turn your entrepreneurial dreams into reality and join the ranks of inspiring young business leaders shaping the future.

I believe in you. Good luck, my young entrepreneur!

Printed in Great Britain
by Amazon

44459818R00091